Survival Handbook for Widows

Ruth Jean Loewinsohn

Survival Handbook for Widows

(and
for relatives
and
friends
who want
to understand)

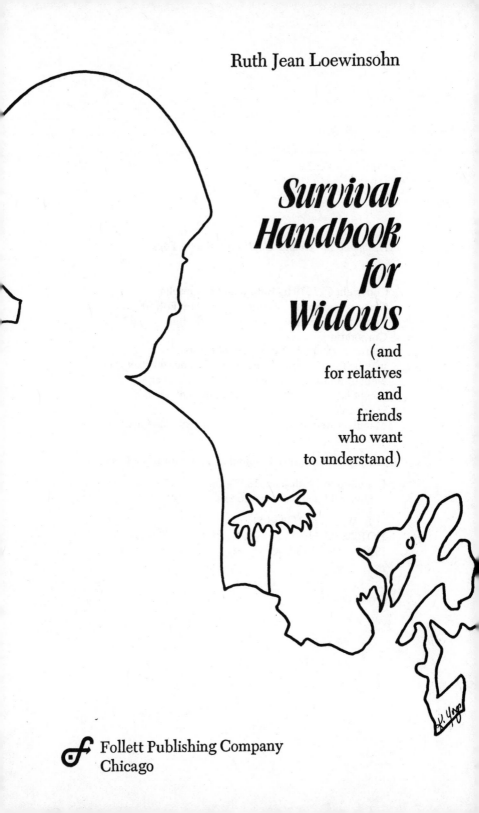

Follett Publishing Company
Chicago

Designed by Donna Cook and Karen Yops

Library of Congress Cataloging in Publication Data

Loewinsohn, Ruth Jean, 1937–
    Survival handbook for widows.

    1. Widows—United States. I.   Title.
HQ1058.5.U5L57   301.42′86   79–11946
ISBN 0-695-81304-8

Second Printing

*This book is
lovingly dedicated
to my children,
Lee
and
Robin*

Contents

Preface

The widow is an often overlooked and an under-understood woman who faces the greatest challenge in her life. She must make sense out of the death of her loved one while carving out a new life for herself.

I have had the special opportunity, in the last six years, of working directly with widows and learning from them what their needs and concerns are. I would like to pass along to you, a new widow, the insights I have gained from the many women who shared their lives with me during these years.

I lost my father when I was a child. My mother remained strong and unflinching, but she never recovered from her loss. I wish she had been able to grieve openly. I think it would have done both of us a lot of good.

In the following chapters, I try to describe the process of grieving that a widow goes through, as well as offer practical ideas and suggestions for coping. I have tried to cover as many phases of the experience of widowhood as possible to show you not only the uniqueness of your personal situation but also how much you have in common with others who have suffered a similar loss.

I wish to thank some of the people who helped me

bring this book to fruition: Irene Brauer, my former secretary, who shared many of her widowed feelings with me; Al Jacobs, a friend who read my earliest ideas and supported me in continuing my work; Leo Baldwin, coordinator of the Widowed Persons Service, who has given my talents room for growth in the past two years; Sandra Reuss, a widow who gave me invaluable criticism and kept me straight; Richard Erlandson, who confirmed my information on financial details; John J. Rockefeller, a widower and friend who supplied me with new insights; Dan Evans, who offered editorial comment; Ron Richard, special friend and confidant; and Gerry Hargrave, who struggled with the typing and retyping of the manuscript.

I also want to thank all the women who shared their lives with me during the past six years. Only some of you will find yourselves quoted, but all of you are here.

I should add that this book was written by a white, middle-class woman who has dealt mostly with white, middle-class American Christians and Jews. There are probably ethnic, racial, and class differences I have not addressed. There may also be differences if family relationships are very close and supportive and differences arising from the area, rural or urban, in which a person lives.

Although the book is about widows, the widower faces many similar problems. The emotions are the same, though the responses, because of societal expectations, may differ. Little has been written about the widower. His needs are as great or greater than those of the widow, since the ability of men to live independently seems more limited by their male role. Thus this work may be helpful to the widower as well.

Chapter 1

But I Don't Want to Be a Widow!

"But I don't want to be a widow!" is the anguished, sometimes hysterical, always plaintive cry of a woman after the death of her husband.

Death may come unexpectedly—heart attack, automobile accident. Death may be anticipated—cancer, emphysema. But the event itself, death itself, is always sudden. None of us is prepared. The reality of the death of a loved one is very hard to accept. Our own feeling of immortality is rudely shattered when a husband dies. Although marriage vows may say "Till death do us part," none of us expects it to happen—at least, not to us.

What happens in the first few days following the death of your spouse? What can you expect of yourself? of others? Let's explore what is known about this time. My hope is that this exploration will help you feel easier about how you are reacting or how you did react in the days following your husband's death.

SHOCK

The first phase of grief is often called impact, or shock, in the scant literature on widowhood. It lasts from a few days to a month or two following the death. During this phase, the body functions to protect the survivor and give her time to accept and adjust to the death.

Persons in a state of shock have been known to do surprising things, totally incomprehensible in terms of their usual behavior. During fires and other crises, such suspended, autonomic functioning sometimes creates heroes. The same kind of behavior is frequent among the newly widowed.

For example, at a funeral I attended a few years ago, a middle-aged woman was comforting her dead husband's sister. The sister-in-law was hysterical, and the widow was holding her and calmly offering soothing words. Some months later, I spoke to the widow about her behavior at the funeral. "How could you be so calm?" I asked, and she shook her head. "I don't know how or why, but I felt I had to be calm, for my husband's sake." The state of shock she was in allowed her to function with seeming calmness and serenity during the public mourning. During this first phase, the widowed person is also often stunned and bewildered. One widow told me, "The numbness was a blessing. By the time I realized what had happened, I had already made the arrangements for the funeral. I didn't think I could make them but I did, because I was numb." Another widow I spoke to wondered when she would begin to hurt. She went through all her usual motions—going to work, coming home, even laughing with friends. About two months later, her hurt began.

DISBELIEF

Frequently, there is disbelief. You cannot truly accept the fact that your spouse has died. One woman, whose husband had had several heart attacks and recovered from each previous one, could not believe that her husband did not recover from his last heart attack. She felt he would get up and move around again if only she waited long enough. She would not allow his body to be removed for at least two hours after the doctor had pronounced him dead.

Often it takes months and sometimes a year or more for emotional acceptance of the reality of the death. Emotional acceptance often takes longer than intellectual acceptance.

In the first few days, you may function as though you were split in two. Part of you may be going through the motions of the funeral while another part of you watches and wonders how you can be so calm. It is normal to dissociate yourself from yourself in order to deal with the pain. By doing this, you keep some control over your emotions until such time as you feel ready to allow them to emerge.

The impact of the death of a spouse is little understood by people who have not been widowed. They feel a person is "so brave" and then can't understand the flood of tears that begins when the initial impact has worn off. Sometimes the widow herself does not understand her behavior.

A classic example of the "heroic widow" was Jacqueline Kennedy. She was obviously functioning in a state of shock throughout the days following President Kennedy's death. Yet on every television set in the country, her "stoic" behavior was lauded. It was assumed that this was the ideal way for a widow to behave. What Americans could not see was Jacqueline Kennedy's reaction after the shock had worn off. This later reaction is normally emotional and much less controlled.

RELIEF

Sometimes widows also feel relieved. Not all marriages are made in heaven. Many relationships continue for the sake of the children, because of neurotic needs, or for financial reasons. When the husband in a troubled marriage dies, his widow usually feels relieved. She will also, however, usually have the other feelings already described—shock and disbelief.

If your husband died of a long-term illness, you may also experience relief.

"My husband was in pain for six months before he finally died. I felt relief when he died, because he was out of his suffering. But when I told others I was relieved, they felt it was sacrilegious or wrong."

"When he was ill for such a long time, it became a drag."

"My shock came when I found out my husband had cancer and that it was terminal. I wasn't in shock when he finally died. I felt only relief."

If your husband suffered a long illness, you have had some time to come to terms with the reality. Although you may never have given up hope, you may have begun to say "good-bye" in many ways before he died.

Because other people expect the widow to be mourning, however, the person who feels relief at the death of someone whom she has watched suffering may be considered callous by uncomprehending friends. They do not understand that to watch a person who was once dynamic lose all his strength is very difficult. The physical and emotional toll that a long illness takes on the spouse is often overlooked. The energy used in taking care of the ill person, in attending to home or business problems, and in sustaining herself leaves the woman drained when her husband finally dies. She sometimes suffers a physical collapse after the long strain has ended.

Relief, along with shock—because even when we are prepared for the death, shock is normal—are therefore often part of the impact of death when the widow has had to deal with terminal illness.

GUILT

Almost all of us also suffer from a feeling of guilt when someone we love dies. This feeling is normal, as we shall see in chapter 7, and almost inescapable. But there are some situations in which this feeling of guilt is intensified. Some widows whose husbands die after a long illness feel guilty because they withdrew emotionally from their husbands before the death. The woman who is not able to stay as close to the dying person as she thinks she should does not realize that her withdrawal is a way of protecting herself from the hurt of the impending loss. Sometimes the dying person also retreats, causing even greater conflict. Dr. Elisabeth Kübler-Ross, in her books on death and dying, deals with these problems. Two of her works are cited in Suggested Readings at the end of this chapter for the benefit of readers who have been forced to cope with such situations.

THE FUNERAL

Adding to all these feelings—shock, disbelief, relief, and guilt—is the stress of the funeral. If there are differences of opinion between the widow and other relatives about how the funeral should be planned or handled, much strain can be created in the family.

Pressure is often put on the widow to plan a funeral more elaborate than she would normally consider. Such pressure comes from relatives to whom an elaborate funeral represents a final honor for the deceased. It may also represent their desire to maintain the family's social status in the community. Sometimes relatives who feel guilty about their behavior toward the dead person seek to assuage their guilt by trying to arrange an opulent funeral. Sometimes the funeral director suggests arrangements that seem unnecessary or overdone.

You, the person closest to your husband, have the clearest understanding of what his wishes were. You also know best what your own needs are. It is hard to stand up to others during this period, when you are confused and in shock. However, if you can identify one relative or close friend who sees things your way and who can give you moral support, latch on! That's what friends and relatives are for.

Even worse than being pressured is being treated as if you don't exist. Plans are made, but you are not consulted. One woman commented, "If only I had been treated like a person instead of an object—if I had been consulted on some of the arrangements. I might have said that I didn't know, but at least I would have been involved. I felt as if everything was going on around me but I had no part in it."

When one person dies, many people are affected. Each one has ideas and feelings about what should be done. Friends and relatives should make a special effort to help you select the funeral arrangements you think most appropriate.

Once the funeral is over, relatives and friends of the deceased often descend on the widow. Reactions to this deluge of humanity may vary. One widow asked, "How can people be so cruel? Everyone came over to the house after the funeral. I suppose that was okay, but they all got drunk and were talking about Joe. I couldn't stand it. I had to get away. Was I wrong not to be a better hostess? How could they!"

Two conflicting parties are involved here: the widow, who did the right thing by leaving, and the friends, who were not really being disrespectful to her or to her dead husband.

Many persons feel that the custom of inviting people home after the funeral is barbaric. It is sometimes hard for the newly widowed woman, who is raw and vulnerable, to bear the trappings of life. How can other people live and eat and drink and laugh? But there is more to Joe's friends' response than cruelty. Just as death is so hard for the widow to accept, it is also hard for others. Because Joe's friends found it hard to accept his death, they may have eaten and drunk too much to help themselves deal with this reality.

Certain religions use the wake or other feast ritual as a commemoration of the life of the person who died. If his friends remembered Joe by telling anecdotes about him, it was their way of commemorating him. The widow's response—leaving—seems appropriate. She is not bound by the conventions of others. Relatives or close friends should have seen that the guests were properly cared for while she rested or found a place where she could be alone for a while.

An interesting sidelight about mourning practices, and the ritualization of them, is that in some primitive tribes, death is followed by twenty-four hours in which the bereaved are allowed and encouraged to engage in any sort of behavior they wish, no matter how unusual or bizarre. The whole tribe wails, moans, and grieves for the dead person. Once the twenty-four hours are over and the mourning is completed, the tribe goes about its business. All have finished their grief work and feel ready to continue living.

Death is an invader. For at least the first few days after your husband's death, as we have seen, you may feel numb, like a zombie, or very calm. You need to understand, as do your friends and relatives, that your initial reaction to the impact of the death is an inescapable one. This first phase of mourning gives you time to adjust to your new status. The next thing you, and they, must understand is that, after the first shock has passed, the real work of grieving begins. "The funeral is the easy part," it has been said. The hard part comes after.

SUGGESTED READINGS

Kübler-Ross, Elisabeth. *On Death and Dying.* New York: Macmillan Publishing Company, Inc., 1969.

———. *Questions and Answers on Death and Dying.* New York: Macmillan Publishing Company, Inc., 1974.

Maryland Center for Public Broadcasting. *Consumer Survival Kit: The Last Rights.* Owing Mills, Md.: Maryland Center for Public Broadcasting, 1976.

Ogg, Elizabeth. *A Death in the Family.* Public Affairs Pamphlet no. 542. New York: Public Affairs Committee, Inc., 1976. (381 Park Ave. S., New York, N.Y. 10116)

Chapter 2

The Loneliness of Silence

A death occurs. The family is drawn together. Grown children come from their homes, often with their own families. Sisters and brothers, aunts and uncles gather. The widow, in shock, accepts their support in a daze. For a couple of weeks, everything possible is done, in most caring families, to cushion the newly bereaved, to make the widowed person's life as comfortable as possible. However, reality dictates that children must return to their own chosen paths of life. Relatives return to far-off states. Friends, although they care, are not as intensely involved as during those first few weeks. To the new widow, who cannot see beyond the loss she has suffered, this is another abandonment—just when she needs people most, when feeling begins to return.

The shock that allowed you to function automatically, or at least to get through somehow, has begun to wear off. The reality begins to dawn on you. *I am alone.*

It may happen suddenly. Mary, already widowed for a month, woke up in the middle of the night, screaming hysterically, "My husband. My husband." Mary had not allowed the awareness of her husband's death to surface before. The shock had not worn off until this moment. When the reality suddenly hit, she cried for hours.

It may come when you turn to tell your husband something about the day's events that you want to share, but he isn't there. Shock or impact is like the novocaine the dentist gives you when he or she pulls a tooth. You are numb while it happens and for a short while afterward, but when the novocaine wears off, *it hurts like hell*. This phase of grief, when the numbness wears off and feeling begins to return, is called recoil.

If other close family members have died—a mother or father while you were still a child, a sister or brother to whom you were attached, or a child of your own— you have experienced the intensity of grief before. Still, many women find that the emotions they experience after their husbands' deaths are the most intense they have ever experienced.

You may be afraid of the intensity of your feelings. Others may also fear the rush of emotions from the widow who "was doing so well at the funeral." Because many people equate intense emotion with loss of control or mental illness, they cannot differentiate between these states and the normal emotions that the new widow feels as she wakes up to the harsh reality of loss.

You will handle your feelings in different ways, depending on your upbringing, what you consider acceptable behavior for yourself, your life-style, your awareness of yourself, and what others who are important to you say about how you "should" deal with feelings.

In the next chapters, I deal with the phase of grief called recoil. The period of recoil is the time during which most of the work of mourning is done. It is a descriptive name. Many different reactions occur during this phase. It is important when reading the following chapters to remember that you may experience any or all of the feelings described. You may also experience emotions not described in the book. The various ways a person responds are all part of the normal grief process as long as they serve the purpose of helping the person work through the loss. Recoil starts when the impact wears off—usually between one and two months after the death—and can last anywhere from six months to two years. Each person has her own way of functioning and her own timetable.

Following are some of the questions I have most frequently been asked about the first months of this little-understood time, when the numbness begins to wear off.

LONELINESS

"What about my feelings of loneliness?"

During the first couple of months, the widow is often very busy. There are forms to fill out, people to see, practical problems to deal with. Loneliness, although there, is masked by the busywork. But loneliness is ever-present.

"Even if I have friends over, I know they will leave soon and I will be alone again."

"I was running on a treadmill—involved with five days of volunteer work—but I was still so lonely."

"I was fortunate I had work to return to, but nights and weekends were awful."

These are only some of the expressions of loneliness that I have heard from the newly widowed. When one widow told me, "I am afraid to stay home alone at night," she giggled in embarrassment. But what she felt was perfectly natural. She had lived with someone for fifteen years and had seldom, if ever, spent a night alone during those years. I know of no way to relieve loneliness. One has to get used to it and become comfortable with it. This takes many, many months to accomplish.

Many widows face exactly this dilemma. They are not supposed to be afraid to be alone—they are told to "buck up," that they are "so strong," and hear all the other clichés—and yet they have no experience with being alone. Somehow, magically, the new widow is supposed to be able to face being alone, to keep a stiff upper lip and, above all, not to show too much pain.

A widow of six months expressed her loneliness to me over and over. She talked about the way she felt when company came over—more lonely and almost wishing they had not come, because she felt so bad when they left. She said she didn't want to impose on her children, yet felt they didn't really understand. She expressed her emotional pain in many ways. I wanted to help. I had an intense desire to find some answer to this woman's distress. Each time I offered a solution, she rejected it. Finally I realized, at gut level, that there was no solution. All advice was rejected *because she was not ready* for the process of recovery to begin—and only she would know when she was ready.

Maybe this is what makes people feel so awkward around newly widowed people—wanting to do something to help or make things better but not knowing what to do or say.

STAYING HOME

"I have been widowed now for four months. At first I seemed to be taking it well, but now I can't seem to adjust. All my friends wonder why I don't get out more, but I have no interest in going anywhere or doing anything. I just want to lie around the house. Can you help me?"

Many widows seem to be handling things quite well at first. The psychological reason for this, explained in chapter 1, is that they are in shock. This is why, quite often, friends are amazed at the composure a widow shows at the funeral. However, after the details of the funeral have been completed, she may become unmotivated and unable to make decisions, cope, or deal with matters about which she has felt competent in the past. During this period, which can last for many months, the most important thing is to recognize that what you feel is normal. Another great help is talking to a friend. Often, someone else who has been widowed can offer support and encouragement. Whatever you do, don't be too hard on yourself. You have undergone a great emotional loss, and your response to the loss is bound to be intense.

Your home may represent security to you, and being among familiar things may be comforting. This feeling of needing to stay home usually passes in a couple of months. The major problem with lying around the house too long is that you can become a recluse. Many women close themselves off completely, shutting out the world. This can lead to an abnormal reluctance to reinvest themselves into the living world. The next question may interest you.

FATIGUE

"I have no energy. I sleep, and yet I'm tired. I feel so drained. What can I do about this?"

You have been through an intense trauma. You have used up all your energy. When you were in shock, your energy was a kind of hyperenergy, coming from the adrenal glands. You were much like people who find extra strength when they have to fight but don't think they can. Now that the shock has worn off, you are worn out—drained. That's okay. Don't fight it. Try as much as you can to take good care of yourself. You are probably not eating well these days. Multivitamins with minerals, as a dietary supplement, might help. Try to eat. If it is too hard to cook, make blender drinks with fruit juices or milk, with an egg and honey thrown in. It takes only a minute to blend a nourishing drink.

Give yourself one small task to do each day. Reward yourself—with sleep, food, or whatever would be a reward to you—for completing the task. Above all, let yourself feel whatever you feel about the death of your spouse. If you suppress your feelings, you will lack energy because whatever energy you have you are unconsciously using to stop your feelings from coming through.

SLEEPING

"I can't seem to get myself up in the morning—there is no reason to get up. All I want to do is sleep. I know this isn't good for me. What can I do?"

Sleeping is really another way of trying to keep reality out. It may be your way of unconsciously avoiding your feeling of loss. It may help if you can plan to do something each day, something you *have* to do. Having to get up for work, for an appointment, or for a class can be a great help, even if you are unable to do well at the work or class assignment. Your self-will, which used to get you up, probably isn't that strong these days, so you need help from outside sources. One new widow I know asked a friend to telephone her each morning at 8:00 A.M. and talk to her until she felt able to get up. This continued for about a month, after which the widow was able to get up on her own. Friends who understand and do not preach are vital to you during these first few months.

INSOMNIA

"I can't sleep—I stay up late and wake up early. I feel so ragged, yet I can't seem to sleep."

Not sleeping, like sleeping too much, is a physical manifestation of the stress you are under. One recently widowed woman put it very succinctly when she told me, "The nights are the worst. I can get through the days, but I'm up pacing the floor at three or four in the morning. Everyone else is asleep except me."

It often helps to call a friend and talk—if you have a friend who stays up late and will listen. My former secretary used to go to sleep, wake up, and not be able to fall asleep again. She took to writing her feelings on a piece of paper, no matter how absurd or scary they seemed. She would carry the paper around with her during the day and reread what she had written. In this way, she finally relieved herself of her feelings and was able to get some sleep.

PHYSICAL PAIN

"I feel a pain in my chest, and I wonder if I am having heart trouble. My husband died of a heart attack, and now I am afraid I am going to die, too. What shall I do?"

The physical pain is real. See your doctor for a complete physical examination. Unless the doctor finds evidence of heart trouble, however, the pain is more likely another reaction to the death of your husband.

Many widowed persons have complained to me of breathlessness, a heaviness in the upper chest, and other symptoms that reflected their grief. The heaviness in the chest area has also been described as a "weight," an "ache," and a "broken heart." There may actually be a physical constriction of that area—a tightening that protects against further loss.

Physical pain, loss of appetite, neglect of self, and lack of motivation are all part and parcel of the reactions associated with the loss of a loved one. They are normal during the first few months after the death.

Unfortunately, most people are too hard on themselves and feel as though they are not functioning well enough or are not living up to the expectations of family and friends. You need to realize that your feelings will be there whether you express them or not.

If you accept what you are experiencing as part of the normal process of grief, you will be more caring of yourself and more willing to allow yourself room to grieve.

There is an axiom in psychology that the unexpressed causes the conflict. I feel that once you admit to a feeling and express it, no matter how bad or wrong the feeling seems to be, that feeling begins to lose its power to control you. This is as true of grief as of any other emotion we experience.

SUGGESTED READINGS

Caine, Lynn. *Widow.* New York: Bantam Books, Inc., 1975.

Peterson, James A. *On Being Alone.* Washington, D.C.: NRTA-AARP, 1978. (1909 K St. NW, Washington, D.C. 20049)

Chapter 3

Sorting Out the Details

The new widow faced with the myriad financial details that accompany a spouse's death must feel like Alice in Wonderland. Alice fell down the rabbit hole and found a bottle that read "Drink me." She drank from the bottle and shrank to ten inches—too small to get the key that opened the door to the garden she wanted to enter. She found a cake that had "Eat me" written on it. She did and grew to ten feet. Then Alice could reach the key, but she could not fit through the door. She did not fit into the world around her.

"What is all this?" "What am I going to do?" "Whom can I talk to?" "Why am I faced with this now?" the widow asks. She feels she must make decisions, decisions, decisions, often with little preparation and even less information. Since financial problems arise in the first months after the death, the widow, who is in emotional turmoil, must set her emotions aside to deal with financial crises.

If you have been lucky, you and your husband discussed finances, and you will have an easier time dealing with the problems discussed in this chapter.

However, many couples avoid discussion of death and

avoid planning for its eventuality. It does eventually happen to each of us. Some believe that if we discuss death, we are inviting it sooner. This myth leaves many widows unprepared for the inevitable.

The barriers are great. It will be a long time before the husband's outmoded idea of "taking care of my little woman"—really leaving her floundering in a financial fiasco—gives way to a working together to understand family resources and plan for all possibilities.

This chapter will deal with what to do, how to obtain the benefits available to you, and what to look for as you move through the financial maze after your husband's death.

FIRST STEPS

The first steps may seem frighteningly difficult. Use the following list as a guide.

1. Find any important papers your husband may have had. You may have to search for them. Important papers include bank books, certificates of deposit, stock certificates, real estate deeds, car title, will, copies of your tax returns for the last seven years, insurance policies, and anything else that looks official. *Do not throw anything out.* It is very easy to feel overwhelmed and give up. More than one frustrated widow has thrown away an old insurance policy only to discover too late that the policy still had a death benefit. One woman felt she was invading her husband's privacy when she looked through his papers. Many widows have described the same queasiness as "snooping." If you don't feel able to search, ask someone you trust to assist you. Often, just the person's presence can be a support.

2. In some states, the bank deposits and safety deposit box contents of the deceased are frozen. If this happens, you will need the proper authorization to have the assets and other valuable papers released.

3. You need a number of certified copies of the death certificate, your marriage certificate (you know that you and your husband were married, but others may require proof), your husband's birth certificate (to establish his age), his military discharge papers, his Social Security card, W-2 forms for the past year, and birth certificates of any minor children. These records are needed to establish claims for Social Security, life insurance, or veterans' benefits.

4. Contact your husband's insurance company or companies. Each insurance company needs a statement of claim (the widow has to ask for the money) and a death certificate or attending physician's statement. Companies may request further proof if they deem it necessary. In any situation where suicide is suspected, there will be need for further verification of the cause of death. The claim must be completed by the person legally entitled to receive the money.

There are various ways in which insurance money may be paid to the widow. Unless all the money from the insurance is needed immediately, options other than a single-sum payment should be explored. Each situation differs. No one choice is best for everyone. If you can discuss these matters with your insurance agent without feeling pushed, do so. You may not understand some of the things the agent is explaining, but you have the right to ask for as much explanation as you need so that the decisions you make are best for you.

5. Apply to your Social Security office for benefits. Social Security benefits are not received automatically; they must be applied for. Specific information about Social Security benefits begins on page 35.

6. If your husband was a veteran, apply for veterans' benefits at the nearest Veterans Administration office. The address can be found in the white pages of the telephone directory under "United States Government."

Specific information about veterans' benefits begins on page 36.

7. Write a formal letter to the company or companies for which your husband worked, his union, professional organizations to which he belonged, and any other group or organization with which he was connected. Inform them of his death and ask for information about group life and health insurance policies, annual leave or sick pay due your husband, special funds, pensions, or any other benefits to which you think you might be entitled. Men often apply for policies as a part of a fraternal organization membership, and they sometimes neglect to tell their wives about these policies. Unless you check, you may be throwing away money due you. You may want to ask a friend to write these letters for you to relieve you of some of this inexorable burden.

8. If your husband had loans, mortgage-service contracts, or credit cards covered by credit life insurance, all or part of the outstanding balance may be payable by the insurance. If there was mortgage insurance, your house will be paid for, and this will be one less worry for you.

You need to advise all creditors—including issuers of charge cards—of the death of your spouse. If credit life insurance was in force, they will know even if you don't. You can ask to see their copies of the original contract to be sure of the situation.

The funeral director, doctors, hospital, or creditors may dun you for payment of bills. Don't ignore them without legal advice. If you are not certain of your finances, a letter to each with a token payment (five dollars monthly is sufficient) will advise them that you intend to pay your bills but need time to determine your financial status.

9. Obtain legal assistance. Your family may be very well-meaning, but they are not lawyers. Find a lawyer you trust who specializes in wills, estates, and probate. Discuss fees before you engage him or her.

Lawyers usually charge by the hour. Therefore, the more you have sorted out before you see the lawyer, the less your cost will be. Bring any papers you think you'll need with you. If the attorney does not explain things to you, ask for the explanation. You have the right to understand fully what is happening to you.

Under the circumstances—you have had a major loss and the last thing you want to deal with is money—you are bound to make mistakes. *Any decisions that can be put off until you feel better emotionally should be.* It may seem to you that you are functioning adequately, but many widows who thought so have decided later that they did some erratic things. Lynn Caine, in the book *Widow,* talks of her move to the New Jersey countryside, which was more than just a financial disaster. Caine was New York City born and bred and realized her mistake a month after her move. She was not emotionally ready to make such an important change in her life. Her move back to the city created even more turmoil. She took action much too quickly, causing many, many problems for herself.

LEGAL TERMINOLOGY

The legal profession uses words that have specific meanings known to lawyers, judges, and paralegal assistants but that are often incomprehensible to the layperson. Following is a list of legal terms most often encountered by widows.

administrator or **administratrix**   the person named by the court to handle the estate if no one was named in the will or if the person who was named cannot serve.

assets money or value in any form owned by the deceased.

beneficiary a person named in the deceased's will to receive assets or who is entitled to them by law.

bequest a gift of personal property given through a will; a legacy.

codicil an addition to a will.

decedent the person who has died.

devise to give real estate through a will.

estate all assets and liabilities left by a person at death.

executor or **executrix** the person or institution named in a will to handle an estate. The executor has a number of functions related to the estate and is paid a commission for his or her work.

holographic will a handwritten will, not always legal.

intestate leaving no will. Each state has specific laws as to how an estate is divided when there is no will.

legacy a bequest.

liabilities money owed.

probate the process by which title is transferred in accordance with a will. Probate is administered by the courts. Its purposes are fourfold: (1) to carry out the desires of the person who died, (2) to transfer title to the assets owned solely by the deceased, (3) to protect creditors, and (4) to protect the beneficiary or beneficiaries. Probate takes time and costs money. It usually takes between nine months and two years, during which time money is tied up. However, there is a provision that allows the executor of the estate to give the family an allowance—enough to live on for a year.

right of dower a widow's life interest in the property of her deceased husband.

trust property or money set aside for a particular person or persons and managed by a trustee for the benefit of the person or persons. There are many types of trusts.

trustee a person or institution that sees to the distribution and handling of a trust.

TAXES

See a tax accountant or tax lawyer to help you, especially during the first year of your widowhood. Under federal law, an estate tax return (no. 706) must be filed within nine months of the death by the executor of every estate with gross assets (assets before any deductions are made) of more than $122,000. Since the tax laws were revised in 1976 and are extremely complicated, expert help is needed to determine your tax liability.

All states except Nevada also impose a state inheritance tax, determined differently in each state. Again, expert help should be sought.

SOCIAL SECURITY

According to *Your New Social Security and Medicare Fact Sheet,* published by the National Retired Teachers Association/American Association of Retired Persons/ Action for Independent Maturity, which reflects changes effective January 1978, if your husband was insured by Social Security, you are entitled to monthly survivor benefits: (1) at the age of sixty-five (sixty if you elect reduced benefits), (2) at any age if you are caring for a child under eighteen or one who is disabled, (3) at fifty if you are totally disabled, (4) if you have unmarried children who are under the age of eighteen (twenty-two if they are full-time students), and (5) if a child becomes disabled before the age of twenty-two. A widow without children cannot receive benefits until age sixty unless she is totally disabled. A widow with children receives no benefits after her youngest child reaches age eighteen, or twenty-two, until she is sixty-five, or sixty.

The fact sheet also indicates that if you work and earn more than the earnings limit, your Social Security is reduced (this does not affect the amount sent you for your children) and that there is a family maximum, a top amount that can be paid monthly to all the survivors together. A lump-sum benefit of $255 is also payable to the widow.

A word or two about remarriage is in order here. In the past, many widows and widowers did not remarry because their Social Security benefits would be reduced if they did and this would create financial hardship. Many older couples lived "in sin" to insure their economic survival. A new Social Security ruling, effective January 1979, allows widows and widowers who remarry after the age of sixty to retain their Social Security benefits at the same level as before their remarriage.

Get in touch with your nearest Social Security office. The people who work there are usually very helpful about processing your claim. If you are having difficulty concentrating, ask a friend to go with you and take notes.

VETERANS' BENEFITS

There is more than one type of veterans' benefit to be aware of:

1. There is a $250 burial allowance for honorably discharged war veterans or veterans of peacetime service with a service-connected disability.

2. Free burial is permitted in a national cemetery where there is space.

3. If your husband is not buried in a national or government cemetery, a "plot allowance" of $150 may be payable.

4. If the veteran's death is service-connected, the allowable amount may go up to a total of $800.

5. Gravestones are available through the Veterans Administration (VA) for honorably discharged veterans.

6. The VA pays a dependency and indemnity compensation to widows of veterans who died in service or from a service-connected disability. The amount is based on your husband's pay grade while he was in the service.

7. If your income is less than $2,600 ($3,800 if you have children), you may qualify for a "death pension" even if your husband did not die of a service-connected disability. Contact your VA insurance division for full particulars.

Have a friend go with you to the VA to help you understand all the jargon. Remember to bring your husband's discharge papers as well as your marriage certificate and your children's birth certificates when you apply for benefits.

OTHER BENEFITS

If your husband worked in the civil service, check with the Civil Service Retirement System. You may be entitled to a survivor's annuity benefit.

If he worked for the railroads, contact the nearest Railroad Retirement Office for information about possible benefits.

Check into your husband's pension plan if he had one.

Ask whether you and your children are still eligible for benefits under your husband's hospital insurance coverage, and if so, until when.

DETERMINING YOUR FINANCIAL NEEDS

Once you have a good idea of what your assets from your husband's estate are, you can take the following steps to determine whether they are sufficient for your needs.

1. Take an inventory of your income-producing assets (any assets that make money for you on a monthly, quarterly, or yearly basis). This will include investments and savings.

2. Appraise the dependability of your income.

3. Determine your annual income—your salary (if you work), your benefits, and your income-producing assets.

4. Determine how much you need to live on—your budget. Most people underestimate their needs. They forget one-time, large expenditures like a new water heater or home repairs and seasonal expenses like Christmas and summer air-conditioning. The best way to determine your budget is to review your checkbook stubs or canceled checks for a full year. (If you had two checkbooks, remember to find all your canceled checks.) Even though the year reflected is the year before your husband's death, you can get some idea of what your expenses are. The more detailed you make this review, the more accurate your assessment will be.

5. If your budget comes to less than your yearly income, you are in luck. If your budget is greater than your income, you have at least two possibilities. First, if you have income-producing assets, you may be able to juggle them to produce more income. Consult a trustworthy financial counselor. If you cannot juggle assets, you need to trim your budget to fit your income. The thing you want to avoid, as much as possible, is dipping into capital—the savings or investments that are producing the income.

In this chapter, I have dealt with the immediate financial questions you may have after your spouse's death. In the next chapter, I discuss other financial problems that you will face in the months ahead. In all financial matters, I hope you will take your time, seek competent help from professionals who know their business and whom you trust, and begin to become more informed yourself so that you make the decisions that are right for *you*.

SUGGESTED READINGS

LIMRA. *What Does She Do Now?* Hartford, Conn.: LIMRA, 1971. (170 Sigovrnay St., Hartford, Conn. 06105)

NRTA/AARP/AIM. *Your New Social Security and Medicare Fact Sheet.* Publication no. PF–12. Washington, D.C.: NRTA/AARP/AIM, July 1978. (1909 K St. NW, Washington, D.C. 20049)

Porter, Sylvia. *Sylvia Porter's Money Book.* New York: Avon Books, 1976.

U.S. Department of Health, Education, and Welfare. *A Woman's Guide to Social Security.* Social Security Administration Publication no. 10127. Washington, D.C.: Government Printing Office, 1977.

U.S. Department of the Treasury. *Federal Tax Guide for Survivors, Executors and Administrators.* Internal Revenue Service Publication no. 559. Washington, D.C.: Government Printing Office, 1977.

Chapter 4

More Details

As a widow, you may face many problems for which you have had little preparation. Many women have not had to deal with creditors, consumer problems, fraud, or con artists. They were protected by their husbands, who took care of financial matters. Even women who did take care of finances will find themselves strangely worried, even though they think they know what they are doing, because their fears undermine their decision-making process.

In this chapter, I would like to offer some thoughts and suggestions for the widow as consumer and as the major manager of her family's money.

CREDIT

It used to be that women had a difficult time getting credit. Credit opportunities and protection have improved recently for women, as well as for men. Two major federal laws protect women from unfair and deceptive credit practices: the 1975 Equal Credit Opportunity Act and the 1974 amended Housing and Community Development Act. A woman should understand what the credit laws mean and do not mean and should understand credit ratings.

A *credit rating* is someone's opinion of a consumer's past use of credit. You may have more than one credit rating, depending on the number of persons who have formed opinions about your credit history. When you were married, if the credit reports were filed only in your husband's name, you have no credit identity of your own.

When establishing a credit rating, you need to know what creditors look for. Stability of income, length of residence, record of employment, current income, and evidence of ability to pay without upsetting other financial responsibilities are usually asked about on credit applications.

Credit bureaus, contrary to popular belief, do not determine the credit ratings of individuals. They furnish information about a person's credit history, and they sell their reports to potential creditors. The creditors use their own scoring methods to develop an individual's credit rating.

If you have reason to feel that a credit bureau does not have accurate information about you, you may review the files held by the credit bureau. The credit bureau must disclose to you all information (except medical facts) in your file if you request it. You may contest adverse information and request a reinvestigation. If the bureau cannot verify unfavorable information, that information must be removed from your file. If no change is made, you have the right to submit a statement of the facts, which must be included in subsequent credit reports.

The recent credit laws prohibit discrimination on the basis of sex, age, and marital status in consumer and mortgage lending. This means that creditors cannot deny credit solely on the basis of marital status. It also means that if your husband was a poor credit risk, and you feel that the stability of your income and your ability to pay make you a good credit risk, you can request creditors who deny you credit on the basis of past credit history (your husband's) to examine your current status.

You should also know that, with certain exceptions, a creditor may not terminate existing credit because of a change in a person's marital status without evidence that the person is unable or unwilling to pay.

Mortgage loans are also easier to obtain for women alone because of the 1974 amended Housing and Community Development Act. If you feel you have been discriminated against by a mortgage lender, write to the Federal Home Loan Bank of New York, 1 World Trade Center, New York, N.Y. 10048, or to the Assistant Secretary for Equal Opportunity, Department of Housing and Urban Development, Washington, D.C. 20410.

Credit should always be used wisely. Many women have grown up with the notion that credit is evil and that only cash should be used. This may be a laudable notion, but when you are alone and the furnace blows out, it is nice to have a credit card that allows you to purchase a new furnace and pay for it over a period of time so that you do not have to dip into capital reserves.

INVESTMENTS

If you have received any money from your husband's estate, I am sure you have been wondering what to do with it. I am also sure that your relatives and friends have all made suggestions about how you should invest your funds.

If you are not knowledgeable about investing, one of the things I suggest is, *don't do anything unless there is an emergency.* Wait until your confusion and your feeling of being overwhelmed lift. They will, even though that may seem a remote possibility to you at this time. In most situations, to do nothing is best. If you take action for the sake of doing something, it is almost invariably the wrong action. You would not have bought a car before you learned to drive. Why buy stocks, bonds, or mutual funds before you have learned about financial matters? A savings account in your local bank where interest can be compounded at 6 percent is one way of investing your money safely until you are more able to make financial decisions. You need time to evaluate what you really want to do.

When you feel more clear, find an *objective* person you can trust—preferably an attorney who understands financial matters, an accountant, or a financial counselor. Discuss your financial situation with him or her. Then make decisions. Even then, take your time.

ESTATE PLANNING

As a widow, you have had to deal with one of the most difficult financial situations there is, the settling of your husband's estate. If there was any money involved, you went through many hours of concern and many hassles. When you feel ready, it would be good for you to look at your own situation and put your affairs in order so that, when you die, your heirs will receive your money with a minimum of expense and taxes.

The first step in estate planning is to have a will. You need a will of your own, unless the will you made jointly with your husband contained provisions in case of his death. Even then, I would suggest that any will you now have be looked at by an attorney to make sure of its validity. If you move to another state, you should have your will rewritten to conform to the laws of the new state.

Trusts are a very useful estate-planning tool. Trusts may also help reduce estate taxes. You may want to review with your life insurance agent the various ways your beneficiary, or beneficiaries, can receive payments. Life insurance can be paid in a lump sum or in a series of installments. Or the choice can be left to your beneficiary.

You should discuss federal estate taxes and state inheritance taxes with your lawyer and possibly other advisors to arrange your affairs to minimize the tax your estate and your beneficiaries would have to pay.

Once you have done your estate planning, update your plans every year, on a specific date, to make sure that what you wanted to happen last year, you still want to happen this year.

FRAUD

This is as good a time as any to warn you about the numerous swindles that are perpetrated on the new widow. You may feel that you are aware and alert, but often in the confusion after the funeral, with many things on your mind, you may find yourself listening to "a good friend of your husband" whom you never met who has "an investment" for you that is "too good to refuse." Refuse it.

Check on anyone who tries to offer you anything, wants to make house repairs at a bargain price, wants to sell you anything, or wants to invest anything for you. If you don't know the person, ask for identification and for the telephone number of the company represented. Check the person out with the company. Check the company out with the Better Business Bureau.

Don't give anyone information about yourself on the phone. You may ask the caller for a phone number and say you will call back. Check the number with the directory to insure that it is in fact a working number for the company the caller claims to represent.

Protecting yourself from being taken in may be something you need to learn. Here are some tips to help you.

1. Learn to say no.
2. Deal with responsible, reliable local dealers or services.
3. Never buy on a door-to-door salesperson's first trip to your home.

4. Don't be afraid to ask what you may think the other person will think are dumb questions. They are cheaper than dumb mistakes.
5. Never buy sight unseen.
6. Read and understand contracts before signing.
7. Check with someone who knows the product before you buy, not after.
8. Stay within your income. Do not be oversold.

Suspect a phony if any of the following apply:

1. You are asked to sign your name—now.
2. The prices are too good to be true.
3. The salesperson discredits others who sell similar products.
4. A cash payment is necessary.
5. The contract has vague or tricky wording.

It is important to know what you can do if you feel you have been cheated. If you complain, it may help others as well as yourself. If you don't, many shady, sloppy practices may be allowed to continue. Check your phone book for the Better Business Bureau and your local consumer protection agency.

As a consumer, you have rights. These rights include being informed, being able to choose, getting good performance from what you buy, having what you buy be safe, and having recourse when you have a problem.

HOUSING

The new widow is often faced with the question of where to live. When her husband dies, the house may seem large and empty. Because of the pressure to "do something," which may be internally generated by the widow who feels a need to make changes or externally instigated by children or other relatives who are concerned about her financial ability to maintain the residence, she feels that she must make an immediate decision about housing. Real estate salespersons often descend upon a widow with offers that seem incredible, considering what the couple paid for the house years before.

A widow I recently interviewed had just this problem. Her sister wanted to know what she was going to do about her house two weeks after her husband died.

You do not need this kind of pressure. Under the circumstances, surely this decision is one that should be put off until *you* feel comfortable about making a move unless there is a pressing need for the money that selling the house will provide.

The psychological meaning of a dwelling is also very important. If your home has had great meaning for you as a couple, it may be very difficult to give it up before you have worked through your grief. If you decide to sell your home, do so when you feel you can let go of the home emotionally. Otherwise you will have a lot of unresolved feelings that will follow you to any new place you select.

Robert Rosefsky, in *Rosefsky's Guide to Financial Security for the Mature Family,* cautions that sentimentality can get the best of us and that a widow with an overly large house could certainly find adequate housing for less. But even he adds, "Is it worth it? Everyone has to decide that for themselves."

If and when you are ready to consider other housing options, read the appropriate section in chapter 12.

EMPLOYMENT

Some women need to find a job soon after their husbands die because income is limited. Others are more fortunate in that enough money was left for them to be comfortable without having to look for employment immediately. Chapter 12 contains tips on looking for a job for the woman who needs or wants to work.

One of the things widows often say in the first few months following their spouses' death is how busy they are with financial problems. I hope that the last two chapters have offered some suggestions to help you so that you can turn your attention to your emotions, which don't seem to go away no matter how busy you are.

SUGGESTED READINGS

Commercial Credit Corp. *Women: To Your Credit.* Baltimore: Commercial Credit Corp., 1977. (For a free copy, write their director of public relations at 300 St. Paul Place, Baltimore, Md. 21202.)

Rosefsky, Robert. *Rosefsky's Guide to Financial Security for the Mature Family.* Chicago: Follett Publishing Company, 1977.

Chapter 5

How Long Do I Keep Feeling Like This?

One of the myths about the loss of a loved one is that a person gets over it in around six weeks. This myth is perpetuated by American society, which places a premium on throwaways—bottles, containers, and people. "If he's gone, why keep thinking about him? Get out, keep busy, and you'll be all right."

Reality is not that simple. A woman who has lived with a mate for many years, or even a few, has invested part of herself in the other person emotionally. Very often the husband is the one person in whom she confided. He may have been her closest companion. Many women who find themselves widowed have had no part of themselves emotionally invested in anything other than their husbands, families, and homes. Upon their husbands' death, they find themselves lost and alone, without anyone who seems to really understand what they are experiencing.

However long these feelings of isolation last, they do eventually lessen. According to most widows I have interviewed, the intensity of the feeling lessens in about six months to two years. The time comes when a remembered song brings a moment of sadness but does

48

not disrupt your whole life, as it seems to in the beginning.

When you are given messages by others that "you should be over this," but you, the widow, do not feel ready to do what is being asked of you, try to stay in touch with your own rhythm. Tell the rest of the world that it takes time, time, time to resolve grief and get over the loss. Be patient with yourself.

In chapter 2, I discussed some of the emotions that women feel as soon as the impact of death wears off. Recoil has many aspects. In this chapter, I shall answer some of the questions asked about the other normal problems and emotions that you may face during this phase, in the first few months after your husband's death.

MORBIDITY

"Why do I keep thinking about how Jim died? I keep remembering the events and want to talk about them. Isn't this morbid?"

Not at all. Part of the grief work is integrating what has happened to you. By retelling the story of your husband's death, you accomplish that task. Abraham Maslow, a humanistic psychologist, speaks of "peak" experiences, experiences we never forget because of their importance to us. You don't usually remember what you did at 4:00 P.M. two weeks ago Thursday, but if anyone asks you to describe your wedding day, or the birth of your first child, you can give a full account of the event. Your husband's death was, in a similar way, a peak experience. You will probably always recall it vividly. Right now, talking about his death helps you make it real. The events connected with it lose their larger-than-life quality as you go over each detail. This need to relive the death of your spouse is another normal, although often-misunderstood and stifled, response to loss.

If others shush you when you want to talk about Jim because "you shouldn't talk about him, you should forget him," try to let them know that it helps you to talk. Recognize that it may be their inability to handle your need, and not your need, that is wrong.

IMAGES

"Why do I feel that my husband is still with me? I sometimes feel I could reach out and touch him. I dream vivid dreams about him. Sometimes, on the street, I think I see him. Why is this?"

First, you should know that 99 percent of the feelings experienced by widowed persons within the first two years after the spouses' death are not crazy. They may feel crazy to you, they may look crazy to others, but they are normal ways of coping with grief.

Specifically, your flash of recognition is a wish for your husband to be alive again. Many widowed persons have felt their spouses' presence after death. It is as though you have incorporated part of your husband into you. His presence is a reflection of that incorporation. Even though your husband will always be with you in your memory, your vivid experiences of him will decrease as you begin to become involved in rebuilding your life without him. One widow told me, "I felt John's presence in my car whenever I became upset with people who were driving stupidly." When he was alive, John expressed annoyance when she became upset while driving. The widow had incorporated his feelings of annoyance and, after his death, she felt as though he were there, reprimanding her as he had when he was alive.

Another expression of similar feelings: "When it is 4:40 or 5:00, I expect my husband home and listen for his van in the driveway. I used to call him when I was going to be late, and I still try to find a phone when I am late, to let him know. But that's silly."

The clue that this is a normal reaction to grief is that,

although the widow senses her husband, she knows that it is "silly." She is aware of the reality, even though the feelings of unreality—her husband's presence—come and go.

INABILITY TO CONCENTRATE

"Why can't I concentrate on anything for more than five minutes? I pick up the paper and put it down. I watch a TV program for two minutes and turn it off. I can't finish work on time because I can't keep my mind on what I have to do next."

Again, your inability to concentrate is part and parcel of your attempt to deal with your loss. Your mind is preoccupied with your husband—his life and, as important, his death. Even though you may try to repress it, the need to make sense out of the loss will emerge. Your preoccupation results in an inability to concentrate. Knowing that this is a part of grief and not castigating yourself because of it is the first step to getting over it.

Writing down tasks that need to be done often aids concentration. Having someone help you decide what needs doing now and what can be put off may help. Talking about your feelings to people who are willing to accept them also helps. In many communities, there are organized programs through which widowed people offer to be available to help the newly widowed. Write NRTA–AARP Widowed Persons Service (WPS) at 1909 K Street NW, Washington, D.C. 20049, for information about programs near you. They have a directory of programs for the widowed of all ages.

CLAUSTROPHOBIA

"I go for drives at 4:00 A.M. I don't eat dinner at home. I feel as if the four walls are going to close in on me. How can I begin to feel like I can stay home?"

Facing loss is so difficult. We use all kinds of ways to

avoid it. We run, we take trips, we sell our house, and still the loss is there. *No one can take away the pain* by running, not even you. Once you accept that, then you can try to learn to live with the pain.

SUICIDAL IMPULSES

"What about my feelings of despair? What have I got to live for?"

Most people who are widowed have had similar thoughts. A very important person is no longer in your life. You are bound to have moments of despair as this reality hits you more and more.

People despair most when they feel their alternatives are limited or that they have no alternatives. Keeping alternatives open and finding new ones is vital to your recovery. A widow who feels the alternatives are too limited may begin to think about suicide.

Many newly widowed think about ending their lives, in a passive kind of way. They take chances they wouldn't normally take, they do not care for themselves physically, and they drive a little too fast or drink a little too much.

However, there is a difference between, "I don't care if I live or die" and "I have absolutely nothing to live for. I'm going to kill myself. I know exactly how I will do it."

You are at high risk. But you have much to live for. If you keep thinking about ending your life, call your local suicide prevention center, crisis center, or mental health center. They have trained personnel—staff and volunteers—who understand your despair. They will be able to help you. If there is no such center in your city, call your doctor or the nearest emergency hospital. Tell them how you are feeling. Be honest. It may save your life. People do care and will help.

I truly feel that every person, both physically and emotionally, has a striving toward life. When a woman is widowed, she wonders about her will to live. Eventually, as a wound heals when the body marshals itself or a fever finally breaks, the striving for life will take over.

It is vitally important that you use whatever resources you have, both within yourself and in your community, to help you through the recoil phase of grief. Most people's despair does lift, and recovery comes.

HILLS AND VALLEYS OF GRIEF

"Some days I do really well. Then I see something that reminds me of him, and I regress. I feel I should be progressing. How can I continue to progress?"

The woman who told me "I regress" did herself an injustice. Your feelings, your memories, and your response to your memories do not get turned off like a water spigot when your glass is full. They will be with you always. The "progress" she spoke of can be best understood as hills and valleys in one's feelings. As you recover, the hills become higher and the valleys less deep.

It pleased me recently to hear one woman, widowed about a year, say, "It's okay for me to still feel emotional from time to time when I talk about him." She recognized, as you can, that having a good cry when you remember your spouse is not only healthy but often cleansing.

Another woman told me, "I thought I was doing well the first eight or nine months. But now I can't go anywhere because I start crying at what I feel are inappropriate times. I can't seem to stop. I thought it's supposed to get better. What's happening to me?"

Her lack of control over her emotions seemed to be of major concern to her. This fear of loss of control arises from a myth of our culture. I'm amazed at how many women accept this stereotype as appropriate for themselves. Men learn to be competitive, never to show how they feel, and to be "strong." If they lose control, they are considered weak, childish, or feminine. Yet many women, too, are terrified when they cry and feel out of control. However, our emotions *will* be expressed.

When she said, "I was doing well for eight or nine months," I can only surmise that she kept tight control over emotions that needed expression. Since they were not allowed expression when they came up, they embarrassed her by forcing their way into her consciousness at times when she wanted to be in control. If you accept your emotions as valid and allow yourself room to cry when you feel like crying, you may find that your emotions become more controllable. This paradox is often hard to understand, but it works. The problem of remaining sane in a society that rewards control over emotional release is one to which no one has found the ultimate answer.

ANNIVERSARIES AND HOLIDAYS

I have frequently been asked, "How can I handle the first anniversary of my husband's death?"

The first anniversary needs to be lived through— somehow. Some women feel best being with relatives or keeping busy. Others find that being alone, experiencing whatever the pain is, is most meaningful. One woman, on a trip to Mexico, realized it was the anniversary of her husband's death only late in the evening because she was so involved during the day. Another woman, from California, went to Reno, where she had often gone with her husband, and relived memories of many trips there with him. Knowing that the time will be difficult and doing whatever you need to get through the day will help.

But how about Christmas, Thanksgiving, your wedding anniversary? Each holiday has a special meaning, in your context as a couple, that makes it much more difficult to go through alone. Although many women attempt to celebrate holidays just as they always have, this can be a major strain for the widow. The first Christmas, Passover, or Thanksgiving is the most difficult. New Year's can be especially traumatic.

It is a commonly held belief that more people become depressed, try to commit suicide, and in other ways cry out in their pain during holiday times. Expectations cause some of the problems. Families want things to be so "good" that they won't let real feelings in. They expect the new widow to refrain from feeling until after the holiday. The strain of keeping things "as they always were in our family" without your husband there becomes unbearable. If everyone would own up to how sad it is that Dad isn't here, there would be a chance to remember, share, and enjoy memories of times past.

I think the most important thing for you, the widow, is to do what *you* need to during holidays. Do not feel pressured by relatives. If you want to cook, do. If you want to go out to eat, do. If you want to forget it's a holiday, do. Let your family know your needs and ask for their support. Some women have found, after the first year, that they begin to develop traditions that reflect who they are now. Doing things differently can be one positive way of dealing with otherwise deadly holidays.

Many women, widowed for three to four years, whom I interviewed feel that the second year of grief is worse than the first. They attribute this to the awareness of the finality of their spouses' death.

In this second year, there may indeed be times when the intensity of your feelings overwhelms you. It is important to remember you have only lived one year without your husband. You lived with him many more. You have lost a person to whom you had a great attachment, whom you loved, with whom you shared life. You will never fully replace that loss. Learning to accommodate to the loss is, according to Dr. Phyllis Silverman, prominent researcher in mutual-help groups, the widow's task.

Learning how to go on is realizing that recovery does

not mean forgetting your husband or the life you shared. It does mean feeling worthwhile as an individual. Recovery does not insure that you won't be lonely or alone anymore. It does mean that you will be able to handle the aloneness without feeling overwhelmed. You may never lose the feeling that you were cheated. Yet you learn to accept what happened to you. Recovery may still mean sad days, though the number and intensity of "bad" days decreases. Above all, recovery means looking toward the future, becoming involved in life in the present, and letting go of the energy you have invested in the past.

SUGGESTED READINGS

Bloomfield, Harold, et al. *How to Survive the Loss of a Love.* New York: Bantam Books, Inc., 1977.

Glick, Ira O., et al. *The First Year of Bereavement.* New York: John Wiley & Sons, Inc., 1974.

Kreis, Bernadine, and Pattie, Alice. *Up from Grief: Patterns of Recovery.* New York: The Seabury Press, Inc., 1969.

Silverman, Phyllis, et al. *Helping Each Other in Widowhood.* New York: Health Sciences Publishing Corp., 1974.

Chapter *6*

Nobody Understands

Because death has been such a taboo topic in American society, we still tend to regard the survivor of death as a person who is somehow tainted. As a widow, you feel different not only because of your own vulnerability but also because of the reactions of others, which often seem harsh, cruel, or just plain ignorant. Often you have no one that you feel will understand you. You have no one to whom you can talk about your crazy thoughts, impulsive actions, and mixed-up feelings. It is even worse for widowers. There are few men who share feelings of grief with one another. The expectation that men will be strong, stalwart, and sturdy gives them little room to express their pain. Perhaps that is one reason the death rate is three times greater among widowers than widows.

It is important for you to realize that others do care, even though they may not know how to express that caring. I often ask women who complain about the treatment they are receiving to remember, if they can for a moment, the time before they were widowed. They blush at the realization that they, too, were often cruel, harsh, or unthinking. The unwidowed seldom think that one day they will experience the grief of widowhood.

There is a great need for education of the unwidowed so that they can begin to understand what life is like for the grieving person.

HISTORICAL PERSPECTIVE

Some of the problem stems from a historical fact of which you may not be aware. In America in 1900, a woman's life span was, on the average, about fifty years. Her husband could expect to live approximately forty-eight years. Women often died while giving birth. The widower who married twice or thrice in his lifetime was not unusual. If a woman's children grew to maturity and her husband died, she often had just a few years to live in her new role as widow. Now, a woman lives, on the average, to seventy-three, while the average male's life span is sixty-seven. The custom is for a woman to marry a man older than herself. The result—a situation that no woman who married "till death do us part" expected. Her whole life has been built around "tea for two" and "a bicycle built for two" and now, since the average age at which women are widowed is fifty-six, she has about seventeen years to live alone as a widow. This increasing number of older women who are alone presents a new challenge to American society.

However, society never seems to be ready for massive sociological and demographic changes until long after they have occurred. In America, more than ten million widows have lived a couple's dream. As one grieving woman I interviewed said, "I always thought I would grow old with my husband." Expectations!

CLERGY, PROFESSIONALS, DOCTORS

One study showed that only 3 percent of widows felt that they received help from clergy. Only 3 percent more felt that professionals helped them!* I quote one

---

* LIAMA Research Report–1970–8 (File 730), LIAMA Research Report–1971–4 (File 730).

intelligent, thoughtful widow who sought out her clergyman about four months after her husband's death. She needed some answers to her anger and bitterness and desperately wanted support and understanding of her negative feelings.

"It was the first time after I had been widowed that I reached out to someone. But I felt put down. When I told the minister I was widowed, he said, 'It must be difficult with three children and a home. My secretary's husband works out of town during the week and is home just on weekends. It must be just as rough for you.'" Even though the minister was trying to be helpful, the widow could not accept his awkward attempt at sympathy.

She continued, "By this statement he showed me he couldn't comprehend what the death of someone you love means. But I still tried to talk to him. I tried to express my anger. He said, almost angrily himself, 'Do you feel you were cheated or something?' He made me feel ashamed of my feelings. We were never able to establish a dialog. That incident set me back many months. If I had had a chance to get these feelings out into the open and find out that they weren't strange or weird and that I wasn't an awful person for thinking them, I would have been much better off."

As a widow, newly pained, she wanted understanding and acceptance of her feelings, however selfish, childish, or uncontrolled they may have appeared to the minister. He, on the other hand, possibly feeling awkward in his attempts to help, was not able to allow her to talk or to sort out her mixed emotions.

Unfortunately, this woman's experience is not unique. Clergy may find the intense emotions the survivor feels just as frightening and difficult to deal with as everyone else. Overly busy, they place the needs of the widowed last on the long list of people needing their support. The seminaries offer few courses to the clergy, and these mainly in the past five years, on death, dying, loss, and

bereavement. Some ministers have had no formal training in dealing with these topics and do not understand
the process a person must go through.

It is vital for you as a widow to realize that going
to church or synagogue may be too difficult at first, even
if you had been a regular attendee before your husband's death. Often, the service reminds you of your
loss. The music, the prayers may be all too painful.
When your minister or rabbi understands this, he can
help you so that you don't add to your grief the guilt over
what you may perceive as weakness or lack of faith.

One woman expressed her feelings as follows: "I find
it very difficult to think that my husband is in a better
place or that this is God's will. I just can't believe that
God would be so cruel." Anger at God is natural in grief.
Those clergy who bide with the bereaved and offer support for the expression of pain, hurt, bitterness, and
anger, even when directed toward God, are a valuable
asset to the newly widowed. If you do not feel you can
talk to your own minister or rabbi, or if you find yourself
rebuffed, ask around. Find a cleric who understands.

Professionals in the behavioral sciences—psychia-
trists, psychologists, social workers, counselors—also
often have problems working with newly widowed persons. Professional helpers are human beings first. Unless
they have had personal experience with death, understand their own feelings about death and their fears
about mortality, and have an understanding of normal
reactions to death, they cannot deal effectively with the
pain and loss the new widow experiences.

One psychologist was seeing a newly widowed
woman and felt the widow was doing well enough after
a few months to terminate treatment with the statement "You're a very strong person, and I know you will
be able to deal with your problems." The new widow
felt she had to "live up" to the psychologist's expectations. When she ran into difficulty later and had to return to therapy, she felt she had "let him down." This

psychologist's lack of knowledge about the grief process and its hills and valleys caused him to push the widow out on her own much too quickly. Many professionals need more knowledge about normal grief—how long it takes and what kind of reactions they can expect at various times during the process—before they can effectively treat the widowed.

Doctors, too, often seem unthinking. Doctors sometimes feel personal failure at the death of a patient, and the pain of the survivor may be a reminder of what they may unconsciously perceive as failure. Doctors may care very much but not know how to help the widow. So they may give her tranquilizers or sleeping pills. Unless medically warranted, the medication can become a needless crutch. Many women have refused drugs because they have recognized the need to avoid numbing their feelings.

There are, of course, many supportive doctors. These are physicians who will listen to the widow, understand her emotional needs, and support her in the direction of growth. They will explain any ailments she is having and will not pooh-pooh her physical complaints.

One widow told me she had felt a constant lump in her throat. She feared cancer. Her doctor, alert to her emotional state, examined her thoroughly. He then explained to her that she did not have cancer and that her physical condition, though real to her, was a reaction to her grief caused by anxiety and that it would eventually go away when the anxiety was dealt with. By treating her complaint as valid, he gave her room to give it up.

It would be wonderful if you, the widow, could let people know what support you need. Usually, though, you don't yourself know if what you are experiencing is normal. You go to the experts—clergymen, psychologists, doctors—and hope they will know how to help.

It is my fervent hope that more courses in how to deal with survivors will emerge from our universities and that the emotional needs of survivors will one day be met appropriately by the people to whom survivors turn. Meanwhile, it may still become essential for you to find help. Some danger signals and some ways of finding the help you need are described on p. 139.

FAMILY AND FRIENDS

As a widow, you may feel that persons close to you—family, friends, and couples—do not behave in the most tactful way. Understanding your changed status and beginning to accept yourself in a single role may help you overcome your feelings of rejection. One widow realized, when she had to fill out a form that asked for her marital status, that she didn't belong to anyone. She felt out of place. She had lost her role as a wife.

While you were married, you and your spouse probably did many things together. Communicating, sharing, caring, even arguing, were done as a couple. Your sense of being cut off from a major source of emotional interaction is compounded by the fact that your peer group has consisted of couples. American society adds to the confusion with discounts for couples, tables for two, and commercials extolling the twosome. Many widows experience their loss as akin to losing a limb. You may have an incomplete, "half a person" feeling.

As you begin to find your own sense of yourself—and this will take time—you will feel less out of place. Meanwhile, look for activities that you can engage in without a male escort. Although you may maintain old friendships, look for new friends who function independently rather than as part of a couple. In this way, you will begin to experience yourself in a new context and begin to function more independently yourself.

When friends don't seem to know what to say to you, when they avoid talking about all sorts of topics when you're present, you can help them realize that you are not a two-headed person just because you are a widow. Knowing that your tears may flow, whether or not they mention your husband, may make it easier for them to share feelings with you.

Most of your friends are used to you as part of a team, just as you yourself were before you were widowed. They find it hard to accept you as an individual. This doesn't help your own feelings of being only half a person. It will help if you speak to your friends and explain that you would appreciate it if they did not treat you so carefully. They need to know that when they avoid mentioning your loss, they are hurting more than helping. As a widow, you gain sensitivity and insights that must be shared with friends. Your friends may not really know how to act with you. They need guidelines as to what you need and want. Don't suffer in silence— let them know how you feel.

Friends want to spare you. Often they will plan parties for major events, such as anniversaries, without inviting you because they feel you would find the occasion too emotionally taxing. One widow reported, "When my friends were celebrating their wedding anniversary, they didn't know whether they should tell me or not. They had a long debate about it. Finally they decided to invite me. I thanked them for being honest. Luckily I had another engagement that evening."

On the other hand, friends and relatives may feel that you should be getting out before you feel you want to. A widow of six months recently told me that she is being hounded by relatives to attend a large family function. She does not feel ready to handle a large gathering, yet her relatives insist that it would be good for her. This kind of pushing can be very destructive. You know yourself better than well-meaning relatives. Although you should be told about and invited to your family's or friends' happy occasions, your right to say no needs to be respected.

ADULT CHILDREN

If you have grown children, you may find yourself at odds with them. Their ideas about what would be best for you may not fit your own needs. Their concern can arise out of love and a sense of responsibility. They fear that you might become too dependent on them, so they want to "set you up" somewhere. Usually, their sense of timing is off. They insist that you make plans and change your life before you are ready. They try to resolve their fears by action. Many children have asked me whether their parent should be grieving "this long" —sometimes only two months after the death.

The care of an older widow may cause disputes. Children suggest that their mother come live with them; only later do they realize that this solution may create more problems than it solves. The mother is even more isolated, for the younger family has its own life-style and the widow feels unneeded or like a nuisance. (Two very good books relating to the problems that adult children and parents face are *Survival Handbook for Children of Aging Parents*, by Dr. Arthur N. Schwartz, and *The Other Generation Gap: The Middle-aged and Their Aging Parents*, by Dr. Stephen Z. Cohen and Bruce Michael Gans.)

Adult children must accept your need to mourn. If the adult children can realize that no answer may be *the* answer, at least for the first few months, it may relieve some of their anxiety. Explain to your children that you have lost your husband, not your mind, and you need to be treated like a vulnerable adult, not a mindless imbecile.

You, too, must understand that your grown children are experiencing grief, pain, and loss. This may be difficult for you to realize, lost as you are in your own inner turmoil. Sharing the pain can relieve some of the burden. Talk to your grown children. Share your pain. Recognize their own pain and their needs.

COUPLES

I have already discussed some of the problems you may have with couples you knew while you were married. These problems sometimes become aggravated. For example, if your relationships with couples were tied to your husband's work, there is even less to talk about once he is dead. Such relationships are based on roles, not on your merits as an individual. Realizing that it is not you, as a person, but the couple's perception of the relationship that is hindering communication may make it easier to face the loss of their friendship.

Sometimes you may find yourself cast in the role of the femme fatale by a friend's wife, and sometimes by the husband as well. One widow was very angry about this. "As if I wanted someone else's property! If I want a man, I'll find my own."

Another widow perceived her married friends' reactions in a different way: "I am aware that I am a reminder to those friends who are married that this could happen to them. 'There but for the grace of God go I!' They don't admit it, but I feel it."

Both comments are valid. Couples fear the sexual freedom they assume you have. They are also threatened by the specter of their own mortality, which is made all too real by your presence. The discomfort of some couples results in the "fifth wheel" syndrome experienced by many widows. Because of your own sensitivity, you feel the awkwardness more profoundly than the couples realize.

"On the couples thing—it was partly their sensitivity and partly my own. I felt different, like I didn't belong. I was the same person. And yet, every time I got together with old friends, they talked about old times. And when they talked about Bud, I would cry—and then they were embarrassed. It made for awkward times."

HELPING OTHERS TO HELP YOU

It seems very difficult for others to learn how to show they care for you. The person who cares often expresses that caring in ways that do not show the real deep-down feeling. Awkward attempts to offer support are well meant but often shockingly naive.

From the reports of hundreds of widows I have talked to, I've put together some of the clichés that I feel most disturb you as a widow and your silent response to each.

"Time will heal." (I can't wait. It hurts *now*.)

"You're too young to be a widow." (I know, but it's not my fault.)

"You're young; you'll marry again." (I can't fathom that right now.)

"Call me for lunch during the week." (It's evenings and weekends that are so lonely.)

"Call me and we'll get together." (I feel too vulnerable to call and possibly be rejected.)

"You're lucky you have children." (Oh, yeah?)

"Well, at least you had twenty good years with him. You should be grateful." (I'm grateful, but I'm still lonely.)

"I understand exactly how you feel." (Oh no, you don't!)

If you have friends or relatives who are awkward with you, realize that they are having problems with your grief. If you can, tell them to do the following:

1. Call often. Tell them that you need their calls more after the first couple of months. Tell them not to expect you to call them, since your energy level may be too low for you to make the effort even though you may need to talk.

2. Offer a specific date to do something with you. Ask them to try to think of your "down" times—evenings and weekends particularly.

3. Feel free to talk with you about your husband. Don't avoid his name. It helps you to deal with reality if you can share memories of your husband with friends or relatives.

4. Realize that although you may seem to be "doing so well," you have a lot of grief to work through.

5. Avoid pitying you. Tell them to imagine being pitied. Ask them to put themselves in the position, for a moment, of having others view them as incomplete. Ask them to care about you but not to pity you.

6. Treat you as a human being, as a real person, not like a china doll or someone without brains.

7. Express their caring. If they feel like crying when talking with you, it's okay. Let them know that crying together is better than avoiding the pain.

8. Say nothing rather than offer naive clichés. They should know that a hug or a squeeze of your hand means more than a hundred ill-chosen words. Tell your friends this.

9. Bring food or invite you to dinner. As one woman said, "I have to eat, but it's so hard to cook."

10. Go for walks with you. Walking is good for depression and will allow you to "walk off" feelings.

Most of us feel awkward around pain or suffering. That, too, is normal. If you are fortunate enough to share moments of pain with your relatives and friends, you will eventually share moments of joy with them as you emerge from your grief.

SUGGESTED READINGS

Cohen, Stephen Z., and Gans, Bruce M. *The Other Generation Gap.* Chicago: Follett Publishing Company, 1977.

Lewis, C. S. *A Grief Observed.* New York: Bantam Books, Inc., 1976. (A widower's response to death.)

Schwartz, Arthur N. *Survival Handbook for Children of Aging Parents.* Chicago: Follett Publishing Company, 1977.

Weatherhead, Leslie D. *The Will of God.* Nashville, Tenn.: Abingdon Press, 1975.

Chapter 7

If Only I Had...

How many times have you said, "If only I had . . ." Widows often feel intense guilt. You may feel guilt about unresolved disagreements, guilt about not being with your beloved when he died, guilt imposed on you by a society that feels your mourning doesn't meet its standards.

Often the refrain is different—"If only he hadn't . . ." —and you feel anger at the husband who worked too hard, didn't take care of himself, drove too fast, or drank too much. And then you feel guilty for feeling angry with him.

What is all this? Why do you feel guilt? Why do you feel anger? How do you use denial in the recoil phase of grief? Let's explore your reactions further.

GUILT

It is important for you to know that feelings of guilt are a normal part of grief. Many bereaved people feel responsible for what happened to their spouses. If you knew that your husband was sometimes in pain and suggested that he go to the doctor but he did not want

69

to bother, you might feel that you should have forced him to. Why? Because it's normal to feel guilty when your spouse dies, and you will find some reason for it.

Responsibility for a spouse's death seems to be one of the plagues of widowed people. "If only I had . . ." "I should have known . . ." The sense that you could somehow have changed the course of another person's life and prevented his death gives you some sense of power. It lets you pretend that the reality wouldn't be, "if only . . ." Since the reality is so hard to accept and makes you feel so helpless, you gain some sense of control by saying, "If only I had . . ." You are saying, in effect, "I had some control, but I blew it."

Before you take on this mantle of guilt, first ask why your husband avoided dealing with his illness. Was he afraid? Some people deny illness until it is too late. Even if you had nagged him, it would have been very difficult to make your husband do anything about his illness unless he himself was motivated.

Perhaps, beneath the feeling of guilt because you did not do more is a sense of frustration, even anger, at the husband who did not go to the doctor sooner. Since being angry at a dead loved one seems to be a "no-no," it is easy to take the anger, turn it into guilt, and place the burden on yourself.

One widow was able to verbalize her anger. "I wasn't angry so much that he died, but I was really angry that he didn't take care of himself." She felt relieved when she expressed this natural feeling. Perhaps you, too, can begin to accept the idea that it is all right for you to be angry at your dead husband even though you love him.

Another widow was troubled because she wasn't with her husband when he died. "I had a headache when I left the hospital in the afternoon. He had a private nurse. She told me to go home. When I called in the evening, they said he was resting as well as could be expected. Then they called and said he was dead. I should have been there. Why didn't I go back to the hospital?" This woman asked an unanswerable question.

She could not have known exactly when her husband would die, yet she felt that she should have been all-powerful and, somehow, known he was about to take his last breath. If you have guilt feelings similar to this woman's, your physical health, your drained state, and your need for a respite have been forgotten in your castigation of yourself.

In the two instances cited, guilt is the reaction of the woman who feels helpless in the face of a situation that she has no way of changing. The feeling of guilt serves a purpose in that it allows you to cope with the situation. Eventually, by talking out your guilt, crying out your guilt, and having someone to help keep reality in focus, you will dissipate your guilt. There was no way you could have changed the situation, no matter what you did. It is all right for you to be the person you are because you can't be anyone else.

Some people believe that those who feel the most guilty are those who had rotten marriages, and that people who had good marriages have nothing to feel guilty about. This is just not true. All marriages contain better and worse moments. In all relationships there is ambivalence. One widow I interviewed was suffering great guilt. She and her husband had had an argument about where they would go that evening. He walked out of the house in a huff. She was called by the police a half hour later; her husband had had a heart attack and died on the street. Although their marriage had been warm and loving, she felt guilty because he died when he did, after an argument.

If there has been no time—this is particularly true in a sudden death—to say good-bye, the widow often feels unfinished. She needs to have some way to tell her dead husband the things she did not say. In chapter 8, you will find an exercise that may help you express your unspoken words.

Our culture's suppression of grief often causes a

widow to hide her feelings of guilt. When a concerned friend told her priest about one woman who was being consumed by guilt, the priest was astonished. "She seems to be doing so well. She attends church every Sunday." Accepting her outward calm, he had not realized the extent of her emotional burden. After he became aware of it, he was able to offer some support to her.

DENIAL OF REALITY

Another way to cope with one's feelings of loss is to deny that anything has really happened. Although you may know, intellectually, that your husband has died, it takes much longer to accept the reality at a gut level—that is, emotionally. Denial is a normal part of grief during recoil. It takes many forms.

For example, you may continue to keep house as though your husband were still there to enjoy it. Friends may think you are crazy. If your husband has been dead a few months, you are probably attempting to recapture him in spirit if not in fact. By doing things as "he would like them," you can deny the reality of his death a little longer. Normally, this magical attempt to keep your husband near wears itself out as you realize that you cannot stop time.

Friends can help by staying in touch with reality with you. For example, when you say, "George always liked this dress on me," a friend's response should be to recognize where you are—"Yes, I know he did"—and then allude to reality: "When you feel ready, maybe we can go to buy some new clothes for you." She has not denied your need to refer to George, but she is making you aware of your need, *when you are ready*, to think about yourself in the present.

You can help yourself accept reality by becoming involved in projects that are related to the present. The past has many pulls, and living in the past can be comforting for a while. However, finding outlets in the present that give you a sense of satisfaction, belonging, and importance can be the best way to let go of the fantasy that your husband is still alive.

Sometimes what looks like recovery can be denial. Keeping super busy, without any time for yourself, running from morning to night, looks to outsiders as though you are adjusting. Usually you are running to avoid thinking about or feeling the pain of your loss. One woman told me she kept running so that she was exhausted by nightfall and could fall asleep more easily.

Other forms of denial can include not talking about your husband or immediately getting rid of all his belongings in an attempt to wipe out the reality. One widow was quite candid about her self-deception. "I didn't use the word *widow* for a year. I didn't want to accept Mike's death, and that was one way of avoiding the realization."

Normally, grief has three phases: impact, recoil, and recovery. People can get stuck in the second phase if they deny the reality totally. For example, after the death of Prince Albert, Queen Victoria not only kept everything in his room as he had left it but also insisted on having his clothes laid out each day and his shaving water brought. This went on for thirty years.

Maintaining the *status quo erat* ("the way things were") for years can be harmful. Denying the reality, postponing the fact of death, is in effect not allowing the natural process of grief to heal you. Any widow who continues to enshrine her husband more than a year after his death is stuck and may need professional help to let go of the past and emerge into the present.

Another form of denial, much more subtle, is mythologizing your husband. You make your dead husband into a saint. This is a normal part of recoil, but it is also a way of denying reality. Your perfect husband loses the flaws of a human being. You tend to give him, instead, superhuman qualities of, for example, goodness, sexual prowess, and kindness. By doing this, you protect yourself from reality—and from any feelings of anger you may have toward your husband. If he was "perfect," "the best man I ever knew," and "an angel," how can you be angry with him for your current situation?

One woman explained how she had made her husband, who was a nice fellow, into a superman. "I would always think about how good he was to me, and I would push out of my consciousness any of the things I used to get frustrated with him about." This woman went on, "I felt I was on the road to recovery when I could remember how angry he used to make me when he was late and he could have been on time, and how he used to annoy me with his demands for dinner at a certain hour. It didn't change the fact that I loved him very much , but it made it easier to let go of him and begin to live for today."

A second quote defines another widow's realization of her husband's humanness. "During a thunderstorm, I opened the door to my garage and found it full of water. The bicycle was floating, leaves were swimming around, and the drain was clogged. I pulled on my husband's parka and his big boots and waded out into the garage with the lightning flashing all about me. I was very angry that my husband was dead and that I had to do all this. Then I remembered that my husband had often been away on business trips and that I had had to do this myself many times when he was alive. I chuckled as I waded through the water." Recovery begins as you are able to demythologize your husband. When you can remember his faults as well as his virtues, you are on the road to working out your grief. The next chapter contains an exercise to help you with this task.

ANGER

Guilt and denial can be ways to avoid anger. Emotions are very complex, and often one emotion is used to cover another that you find too difficult to accept in yourself—in this case, anger.

Thus, even though your husband did not die on purpose, you may find yourself feeling angry and then feeling guilty because you feel angry at him, at your situation, at everyone, and at everything.

When your husband died, he left you alone. Although, given a chance, he would not have wanted to leave you, the reality is that he is gone and that you have been left. If your husband were still alive and had walked out on you, you would probably feel intense anger. But you would feel justified because you were "done wrong." In effect, your husband's death is abandonment, and your anger is valid. The only difference is that the abandonment was involuntary; he didn't mean to do it. Unfortunately, feelings inside us are often the same whether the other person meant to leave or not. The most healthy way to handle your anger is to let yourself experience it. Then find constructive ways of working it off.

One recently widowed woman talked to her dead husband's picture and told him how angry she was at being left. Other possibilities include talking out the feelings with a friend who is willing to let you let off steam and who does not tell you that "you shouldn't feel that way." Writing out your feelings in a journal that records your changes in mood can chart your path to recovery. Screaming, hitting pillows, and walking or running off the anger can all be constructive ways of dealing with your feelings.

Avoid turning your anger inward. Women who do not express their angry feelings may escape into drugs or alcohol. It's easy to do. It's hard to work anger out. Giving yourself permission to feel anger during recoil is vital. Anger may be directed at doctors, nurses, or the hospital. Because of the institutional nature of hospitals, a widow's concern that the deceased did not receive enough personal care is often expressed in anger.

Friends are often a target of anger; imagined slights are magnified. Sometimes family members say or do things that infuriate you. The same things, said when you were not vulnerable, might not have had an effect.

Your anger might also be directed at God. Many people have been taught that God is love. Your feelings of pain, loss, and anger at being left may be psychologically in conflict with your religious upbringing. I have consulted many members of the clergy about this. One enlightened minister said, "It's okay to be angry at God. He can take care of Himself. He has broad shoulders and can handle a widow's anger. She has a right to be angry. This is what she needs to feel right now. Whatever your religious beliefs about an afterlife, right here on earth it's hard to be left."

Anger is often related to a feeling of having been cheated. One woman summed up this feeling by saying, "He worked so hard. We were going to retire and travel. Then he died, damn him."

The utter frustration of having to handle things your husband used to deal with, of having to make decisions completely on your own, and of feeling that you are unable to be as strong as people expect all cause anger. Most widows were raised to expect that a husband would care for her forever and ever. When that dream is shattered, it will naturally cause anger. Beneath the anger there may be fear—fear as to whether you can handle it all and fear of taking charge of your life. One widow confided, "Overwhelming—the feelings are so new, so unlike anything I ever knew before. So much anger, crying at the slightest thing or at nothing—how do I do this, how *can* I do that?"

Knowing that anger can be a motivating force can help. If you get angry enough, you may decide to show your husband that you *can* make it. It may be the one challenge that makes you begin to take an interest in life again. Later, you may do things for yourself, not for your husband, and take pride in the fact that you are capable of directing your own life.

If a person has lost other family members and has not resolved the feelings about these losses, the death of the spouse can be the last straw. The anger felt at the loss is intensified, compounded by the unexpressed anger at the previous losses. This anger may be related to more deeply rooted feelings of abandonment or loss that a husband's death serves to reactivate. These need to be dealt with so that one's emotional growth is not stunted.

In this chapter, I have focused on three emotions that can cause you much anguish during recoil: guilt, denial, and anger. They are interrelated emotions, and understanding their connectedness can help you understand your reactions. If you can get in touch with the anger that may rest beneath your feelings of guilt and your denial of reality, if you can give yourself permission to feel the anger and work through it, you may find it possible to begin to say good-bye.

SUGGESTED READINGS

Grollman, Earl A. *Living—When a Loved One Has Died.* Boston: Beacon Press, 1977.

Silverman, Phyllis, et al. *Helping Each Other in Widowhood.* New York: Health Sciences Publishing Corp., 1974.

Chapter *8*

Saying Good-bye: Three Exercises for Letting Go

Your husband has been dead for a year or more. Have you really said good-bye? You and you alone know when you are ready to say good-bye. But this letting go is vital to the development of your own life as a single person. Elisabeth Kübler-Ross, in *Death: The Final Stage of Growth*, writes: "The ultimate goal of grief work is to remember without emotional pain and to be able to reinvest emotional surpluses. Grief work begins with acceptance, with facing up." The key here is pain. You may feel emotional. You may shed tears. You may have memories. But you will not be devastated by the pain of the memories. Kübler-Ross continues: "What appears to be acceptance can be very deceptive and very destructive when the acceptance is only intellectual."

The intellectual acceptance of the death of your husband comes, as I have pointed out, more quickly than the emotional acceptance. One older woman put this so well when she said, "I didn't realize until yesterday [one year later] that I had not fully accepted my husband's death. I would hear him and imagine him in every room.

78

Yesterday I realized that this was my way of denying his death emotionally."

How do you say good-bye? How do you let go of your spouse, of your dreams, of your expectations? The idea of giving up your dead spouse, of letting go, frightens many widows. "You are asking me to stop being married—to forget the most vital years of my life. I won't do it!" This is not what "letting go" means. What I see in the letting-go process is the emotional completion of a life situation that has in fact ended. You are no longer married, even though in your heart and mind you will always treasure the memory of your marriage and all it meant to you. The finite end of a life, that of your husband, is a reality. This reality must be faced, both emotionally and intellectually, if you are to live in the present. Those people who get stuck have lost the capacity to live in the present. But the present, with all its pain and hardship, is the only valid reality we have. The past, with our memories and dreams, needs to be put into perspective.

Of course, you still feel moments of intense emotion when you think of an especially meaningful time in your past with your spouse. Reality can be sad. Yet it is much more comforting than denial, which drains energy from you. Memories are very important, but they do no good if they are used as a shield against the present. Although a new widow may continue to keep house for a few months as her husband liked the house kept, reality soon causes her to pause to consider what her own housekeeping needs are. The stuck widow will keep the house as her husband desired years after it is appropriate or makes any sense. She may continue to live in a house that no longer meets her needs but provides a way for her to stay attached to her deceased husband. In order to let go, the first thing to realize is that you are holding on to your husband only in your mind. In reality, he is dead. This is not meant to be harsh but rather to point up the psychological truth that since how you view your spouse is within you, only you have the power to let go, to say good-bye. No one can say magic words that will cause you to let go; only you can take that responsibility.

But you ask, "How do I say it?"

Three exercises that may help you say good-bye to your deceased spouse follow. The second and third ones are better done with a close and good friend for support. (To the friend: Just be there. Do not try to stop the process the widow must go through. Support her even if her words surprise you. She needs your support and caring. She is strong enough to let go, with that help.) These exercises should be tried only when you feel that you are willing to say good-bye to your spouse. They are based on the belief that one can complete a life situation and go on with one's life in the present. Each exercise may be done over and over, since saying good-bye is a process and not a one-time experience. Engage in the exercises separately, one at a time, as you feel ready.

EXERCISE 1: PERSPECTIVE

Give yourself time and a quiet space for this exercise. On one side of a sheet of paper divided in half, write down the things you admired, respected, or liked about your husband. This should be easy, but please stop when you have listed ten items. Feel free to put down less, but more will destroy the usefulness of the exercise.

On the other half of the paper, write down the things you disliked, did not admire, or did not respect about your husband. Be truthful with yourself. You need not show the paper to anyone else. Try to put down ten items, even though, as you read these words, you may not feel you have any negative feelings to express.

While you are writing out your lists, you may find

yourself becoming emotional. Let yourself experience your emotions. Express them out loud if you can, or write them down. Don't feel foolish talking to an empty room. I have often told clients that the mind works like a pressure cooker—if the emotions inside are not allowed to escape little by little, they will explode. So allow the feelings out.

Now, take the piece of paper, fold it up, and put it in your purse or pocket. The next time you begin to extol the saintly virtues of your spouse, put your hand in your purse or pocket, take the paper out, and reread it. You will soon recognize that your spouse was a real person, with real faults and real virtues, who is now dead.

EXERCISE 2: UNFINISHED BUSINESS FANTASY

This exercise is useful for completing your good-byes to any person who made an impact in your life, not only your husband. It is especially helpful if your husband died suddenly and you feel that there are things that you weren't able to say to him before he died. These unspoken words may be said to the deceased during the fantasy, if you choose.

For this exercise, you need an understanding friend who will read the following to you so you can concentrate on it. (To the friend: Pause for a moment when you get to the ellipses.) "Close your eyes. We are going to take a trip. Take some deep breaths. . . . Imagine yourself going far away, to a mountaintop where you can look into space. Look into space at all the stars and galaxies. Feel yourself at peace on the mountaintop. . . . Now start coming back from the mountain and imagine yourself on a train platform. . . . Trains are coming and going, but you are waiting for a special train. . . . Imagine the train coming toward you very slowly. The train is your life, and each car of the train is a year of your life. Watch as each car slowly goes by, as each year of your life goes by. Whenever you want to, you can stop the train, and anyone you want can get off. When you stop the train at any year of your life, have whoever it is you want to talk to get off the train. . . . Now you can talk to that person and say anything you want to. Things you never said, unfinished business, a joke you may want to share, whatever. Take a few minutes to talk." [Allow a few minutes.]

"When you have finished talking to the person, say good-bye. . . . Imagine yourself putting your hand on the person's shoulder. Turn him around and put him back on the train. Watch as the train starts moving again."

End of fantasy.

This exercise allows you to tell your spouse what you wanted to say but had no chance to. You can bring back the train whenever you need to say other unsaid things.

EXERCISE 3: SAYING GOOD-BYE
THE GESTALT WAY

This exercise should not be done before Exercise 1.

One principle of Gestalt psychotherapy is that until a person completes the gestalt (finishes the situation), she cannot go on to other situations. The work of Gestalt therapists consists, in part, of helping people to get in touch with their feelings and to confront their fears. The theory is that this will enable them to complete the unfinished situations in their lives.

For this exercise, you need two chairs. Have them face one another. Sit in one chair and imagine your husband in the second chair. Although this may seem silly or contrived, remember that it is a technique to help you get in touch with yourself—to help you say good-bye. Begin to talk to your husband. Tell him that you are saying good-bye. Going back to Exercise 1, read him your list of his good points and faults. Say good-bye to each—first a good point, then a fault.

For example: "Edward, I want to say good-bye. I want to say good-bye to your strength, which has helped me through many situations. I will always remember your strength, but I can't lean on it anymore. Good-bye, Edward's strength.

"Edward, I want to say good-bye to your snoring. I am sorry that you died, but I am very glad to say good-bye to your snoring."

As you go through this process, you will most likely experience stong emotions. It is hard to let go. You may cry a great deal. However, you may also experience anger, sadness, laughter—all kinds of emotions. Let yourself experience these feelings as fully as you can, but do not force them. They will come. When you have said good-bye to each of your spouse's "good" and "bad" parts, say good-bye to him as a complete person. This will be hard, yet it is necessary to complete the gestalt. You may need to go through this exercise more than once to get to the end. If you find yourself unable to complete the exercise, stop and try it again when you feel ready.

Each of these exercises is a way to get to what I feel is the heart of recovery for the widow. Many women have let go or said good-bye in other ways. It took one woman I know three years to be able to read the letters that she had received from her spouse when she had been away from him during part of his final illness. She had read each letter when she received it and had written to her husband each day. After his death, the bundle of letters remained among her keepsakes. When she finally felt ready to say good-bye, she sat down one day, took the phone off the hook so as not to be disturbed, and reread each letter. She cried hot, bitter, sad tears, and let go. She was drained when she finished reading, but she felt that her husband was truly dead. She had finally said good-bye.

SUGGESTED READINGS

Baldwin, Christina. *One to One: Self-Understanding Through Journal Writing.* New York: M. Evans & Company, 1977.

Kübler-Ross, Elisabeth, ed. *Death: The Final Stage of Growth.* Englewood Cliffs, N.J.: Prentice-Hall, Inc., 1975.

Temes, Roberta. *Living with an Empty Chair: A Guide Through Grief.* Amherst, Mass.: Mandala Press, 1977.

Chapter 9

The Children Keep Asking, "Where's Daddy?"

A child who loses a parent feels that the world has collapsed without reason. Children may feel that they have been left because of something they did or didn't do, say, or think. They may feel abandoned. They may feel guilty about what they think they did that caused the death. Yet adults often say, "Oh, they will get over it. Kids are so resilient." I wonder. For a child to come to grips with the loss of a parent takes time, openness on the part of the surviving parent, and acceptance of the child's need to mourn. Children do not grieve in the same way adults do. They find ways of expressing grief that may confound and amaze the adults around them.

EXPLAINING DEATH TO THE YOUNGER CHILD

One four-year-old, having seen her father's grave, was still unable to comprehend the finality of death. She expressed her frustration and grief by pounding on her mother's stomach and crying, "It's your fault Daddy died." Her astounded mother asked, "Why is it my fault?" The sobbing child said, "Because you didn't

85

water Daddy. If you had watered his grave, he would have grown again like the plants do."

Although this story may make you smile, it points out the way children younger than six think. Children of preschool age see the world in concrete terms. They do not fathom abstract concepts.

Young children explore the world with their fingers, tongues, eyes—they use their senses. Words are abstract concepts that children understand only as they grow older. The world of young children is based on the concrete reality of what they see and hear. If you tell preschool children to run down to the store or hop into the car, they will probably do just that. Understanding the way they normally think may help you understand how to explain death to them.

One reason most authorities on child behavior are concerned about religious discussions of death with young children is that they have found that the child who is told that "God has decided He wanted your father to be with Him" may take the statement literally. The child may think, "What happens if He decides He wants me?" Or "What if He wants Mother? What will happen to me then?" The child's unspoken concern may lead to unusual or disturbing behavior that the child cannot explain to the parent in a logical, understandable way.

Religion can be a support to adults. In talking with children about death, however, there is need to deal with the reality as well. A child should be told that a dead person does not breathe, eat, or sleep so that the child is not confused about what death means. One woman, when asked how she handled her husband's death with her young children, put it beautifully: "I talked to them with simplicity and truth wrapped in love and assurance."

Even though you explain death this way to preschool children, they may not completely understand your explanation. They have no concept of permanence. They think that if Daddy went to the hospital and doesn't come home, that is just for now. Eventually, he will come home. Therefore, parents are often surprised, after they have carefully explained death to a young child, to hear the child, a few weeks later, quite seriously ask, "When is Daddy coming home?" If possible, the parent should remain unperturbed and explain, again, "Daddy is dead. Daddy will not be coming home. Daddy loves you." This may need to be repeated each time the pre-schooler asks.

INVOLVEMENT IN MOURNING RITUALS

Children should be involved as much as they want to be in the family mourning. The child who is shunted off to relatives during the funeral and after without receiving any explanation of what is happening finds the death more difficult to understand. At a time when children have lost so much, they should not be made to feel un-wanted or in the way.

Knowing that the child has suffered a loss and has to make sense out of it helps you see that the child should be involved. The child's natural curiosity will be a help in making sense out of what is happening. Because of that curiosity, it is important that what is happening during the rituals be explained. A child makes better sense out of a funeral, a wake, sitting shiva, or other ritual if there is someone to talk to about the experience. That some-one need not be the surviving parent or other relative if either is too distraught. An understanding close friend that the child trusts can provide this support by being "assigned" to the child and being with that child throughout the ceremonies and mourning rituals, ex-plaining and answering the child's questions patiently, accurately, and simply.

When the surviving parent cannot cope with the presence of her child at the funeral, perhaps a relative can take charge of the child elsewhere. It is impossible to offer hard-and-fast rules because there is a delicate balance between the parent's emotional state and the child's need to be involved. If for some reason the child is not involved in the funeral, other ways to say "good-bye" to the father have to be found.

More important than whether the child attends the funeral or not is whether the child is made to feel involved. The child is grieving and should be included in whatever way seems appropriate both to the child and the parent.

Often, concern is expressed about whether children should go to the cemetery. Again, this is an individual matter, depending on the child and the parent. I think children should know where their fathers are physically buried. It helps them deal with the reality. A visit to the cemetery often answers all kinds of questions the child may have about where the father is. Once relieved, the child may not wish to go again. Many widows find that they do not wish to go to the cemetery often. Others find some comfort in visiting the grave, at least for a while. The children should be consulted about whether they want to go and should be allowed to go or to stay home.

Cemetery visits can be used positively or negatively. They are positive in that they show the child where the parent is buried. Visits to pay respect may be appropriate. But weekly pilgrimages should be avoided.

PARENT SHOWING GRIEF

Mothers often feel that they must protect their children from emotional storms. The idea is not dissimilar to that of avoiding arguments in front of children when you were married. Yet in counseling adults who lost one parent when they were children, I have found that they often question why their surviving parent was so unreal with them even though they could hear sobs coming from the bedroom. The child's own grief was not given room for expression because the parent was so stalwart. Although hysteria and uncontrolled emotion may be very frightening to a child, normal displays of emotion are reassuring to them. Once your tears have subsided, perhaps you can tell your children that you cry because you remember their father and miss him just as they do. That is an understandable reason to cry and will offer the children room to express their own feelings about their father's being dead. One child's mother broke down at the funeral but later regained her calm, though she was seething inwardly. The child told her mother, "I like your funeral face better."

Remember that you are a model for your children. If, by suppressing your grief, you suggest that grief is embarrassing or should be repressed, you are setting the stage for your children to deny their feelings, which may then be expressed in deviant ways. Although you feel you need to be strong, you may be giving your children an image impossible to live up to. It may be better to show your feelings in front of your children and to allow them to comfort you and offer support, just as you comfort them in their hurt.

THE CHILD'S FEARS

Children become fearful for reasons you may not be able to fathom unless you understand how they think.

I said earlier that preschool children think concretely. They often have fears of monsters. These creatures are very real to children and cannot be explained away. Accepting the fears as valid is the first step in helping the child. If young children have fears connected with sleep, they may be afraid of falling asleep and dying. There has been one death already. Young children need to be comforted and, according to one theory, it helps if they confront their fears. For example, if the child sees a monster, you might suggest that the child talk to the monster and find out what it wants. Then the child can either invite the monster to come to bed, thus making friends with it, or tell it to go away because the child has to get some sleep. It is paramount that the fears not be pooh-poohed. *They are real to the child.* After you have accepted that, you can help the child deal with them.

Because older children, five to ten, think magically, things that are coincidental can become joined. Basically, magical thinking gives children power over their universe. A child might do a snow dance to cause snow. If it snows, the child is sure it was because he or she did the dance. In the same way, children's fears may be related to something they think they did. They may feel responsible for their father's death. Talk with them, assure them that they were not in any way responsible, and hear them out.

Another fear children often have is that they may die the same way the parent did. Since children are often told how much they look or act like a parent, they identify with the parent to the point that if the parent dies, they think they may, also. This fear has to be verbalized, by the surviving parent if necessary. She might say, "I bet you're worried about getting sick like Daddy did." Then she must be ready to listen. Reassurance, once the fears are expressed, will help the child. Above all, however, do not reject the fears. Accept them; then offer reassurance.

Another often-expressed fear is that the surviving parent will also die. A mother may wonder why a child who has been outgoing suddenly begins to cling to her, rarely letting her out of sight. She may become short with the child, upbraiding him or her for being so shy. If she can understand the fear, she can reassure the child that she has no intention of dying and leaving him. The way she says this is very important. A parent who says, "I will never leave you," is not being truthful. A more realistic way of reassuring the child would be to say, "I will do all in my power to stay with you. I am in good health and will take good care of myself. I want to stay alive a long time, just like you do."

If a parent cannot be detached enough to help her child because her own pain and loss are so intense, it may be helpful to find a mental health clinic, family service agency, or private therapist that specializes in play therapy with children. Through play, children may often express concerns they cannot express directly.

TALKING ABOUT DADDY

Widows often wonder whether it is better to talk about their husbands to their children or whether it is better to avoid talking about the fathers so as not to upset the children. Although they do not want the children to forget their fathers, they do not know how much or what to say.

Children are very curious. When somebody dies, they don't really understand the finality of it. Do any of us? We often tend to shield children by not talking about the dead person, but the result is that they feel there is something terribly wrong because no one talks about it.

Children need to be able to talk about their fathers. They need to be able to reminisce. We think of older adults as reminiscing, but children also do. My nine- and eleven-year-old children reminisce back to when they were four and six and even younger. When your children ask about their father, take time to sit with them and answer their questions. You may want to bring up times with your husband when the children were involved.

Often a scrapbook, photograph album, or family story album can be put together with the help of the children. They can tell their stories, as they remember them, of events that they shared with their father. You can write the stories in the album for them if they are too young.

You can talk about how you and your husband met. You can remember for them times that they were too young to remember. If tears are shed while you are working on the album, they are shared tears. Don't be afraid of them.

The most important thing is not to make an angel out of your husband but to answer the children's questions as openly as you can. Try not to make their father into a perfect person. Children need to remember, not worship. The more they can understand about your husband's life, the more they will remember him as a total person and the fewer problems they will have about accepting his death.

OTHER PROBLEMS OF SCHOOLCHILDREN

Ambivalence

Since children, like adults, are ambivalent about people, there may be times when your child does not appear to be affected by the death of his or her father, or the child may even, if allowed, express some positive feelings about the death. One six-year-old said she was glad her daddy died because he didn't spank her anymore. Her mother had a hard time not spanking her herself when she heard her daughter say this. She and I discussed how necessary it was for her daughter to be able to express *all* her feelings without feeling guilty, just as the adult survivor needs to be able to express anger, frustration, and hurt. Her daughter needed to find some meaning in the death and looked for the positive aspects of it to try to make it more acceptable. At some other moment, her daughter might feel angry at her father for leaving, sad because he is not there to hug, or nonchalant as she plays with her friends and for the moment does not think about him. What is important is for the widow to accept her daughter's ambivalent feelings as normal.

Children live mainly in the here and now. That is why

adults may assume that the child is not feeling grief. When you understand the child's ways of relating in the present, you can give your child room to grieve in the child's own way.

Peer Pressure

Parents are often unaware of the pressures put on children by other children. Peer pressure is greatest from the ages of seven or eight and continues to be important through adolescence. What other children do or have is important to your child. Being different from other children is hard to bear. One widow wondered why her eight-year-old never talked to outsiders about his father's death. Although he admitted to her that he knew his father was dead and expressed his sadness about the death at home, he didn't admit to his classmates or to his other acquaintances that his father was dead. Because he wanted to fit in so badly, he avoided talking about it so that he would feel less different from the other children. Understanding his need to do this, his mother did not feel she had to object to his behavior. Instead, she told him that she recognized how important it was for him to feel like the other kids. When he felt that she understood, he did not feel as guilty about lying to himself and others.

Male Role Models

Some widows are overly concerned about their sons' having males with whom to identify. The coordinator of a program for the widowed with whom I raised this question felt that most widows blow this fear out of proportion. Her child had found his own way to cope with the lack of a father figure. He latched on to a friend's father, who became his model. In this widow's opinion, boys will find models to identify with on their own. She felt that introducing a Big Brother, for example, during the first year might be inappropriate, since it would point up the boy's differentness from his friends.

You may want to encourage your son to find a male model by inviting male relatives you admire to come around and take an interest in the boy. However, the relationship should be based on mutual interests and not be something artificially imposed on either the child or the relative.

Discipline

Often, during the first few weeks after the death, household routines are disrupted, and no discipline is enforced. You may feel you cannot deal with any crises, large or small.

You may then become concerned about not setting standards for your children. If this happens, you may overreact by being too strict or authoritarian. It is important to try to return to a routine as soon as possible. But you cannot be both parents to your child. Because of your overconcern about being a good mother, you will have to watch your tendency to either overindulge your children or to be too strict with them. Children need as much consistency as possible. Since, in your grief, you do not feel consistent yourself, it may be very difficult for you to be consistent with them. Remember that you are not perfect. You will make mistakes with your children. Being a single parent is much different from being one of two parents. However, you will not harm your children if you are open with them about your concerns and if you give them as much love and attention as you can without denying yourself your own space and time.

PREADOLESCENTS AND ADOLESCENTS

Preadolescent and adolescent children express grief in ways that adults find incomprehensible. Older children understand the finality of death more clearly, but they have to deal with their grief in ways appropriate to their age. They often express their grief in action, not words.

They may run and run and run. One mother, trying to comprehend her twelve-year-old's behavior, asked, "Why does he keep playing the drums?" The drums were his release.

One therapist I know, who works with preadolescents and adolescents, plays basketball with the kids in order to help them work out their aggression and hostility. He does not use verbal forms of therapy; he uses his relationship and activity with the children to help them. A widow may not wish to play basketball in order to help her son. But if she understands that her son is working out his grief by playing basketball, she may be more understanding of his need to be constantly in motion.

Preteen and teenage boys often get a notion that they have to be the man of the family. Relatives often say to the boy, "Be brave. You must be the man now." Children take such comments literally.

Sometimes the mother herself puts a burden on her adolescent son. She may make him her confidant. She may subtly indicate that her son is the only person she can talk to, a good companion to her, and her salvation. The child who is faced with such demands will be in emotional turmoil. Just as you cannot make up to your child for his father's death, you cannot look to your child to take your husband's place. Once a woman realizes she is doing this, she must back off and give the child room to be himself, not a carbon copy of her husband.

If you find your son at the head of the table, move him back to his own seat. It is vital that the child who is burdened by the loss of his father not feel that he must take his father's place. Often, when this is discussed with a child who has been trying to act manly and he is told, firmly but gently, that he can act his own age and does not need to take over, there is an audible sigh of relief.

Adolescence is the time when the no-longer-child is the not-yet-adult. The adolescent's physical and emotional selves are already in turmoil. Adolescents experi-

ment with emotional independence, sexual interests, and
with their sense of themselves as worthwhile. They demand more freedom and respect, while having new potentialities for delinquency and for making mistakes.
Add to this the death of a parent, and the pressure on
the adolescent is intense.

Often, teenagers cannot talk about feelings. They
may very likely act out their feelings instead of talking
with you. You may feel rejected by your teenager's
unwillingness to communicate with you. It may be
that your child talks with other teenagers about feelings.
Give your teenagers space. Do not feel that they have
to share their grief with you. Do give them an opportunity to talk. You might say, "I feel very sad about
Dad's death. I know you must feel a great deal of pain
also. If you want to talk, I'm available." If you hide your
grief, adolescents may feel they must hide their grief,
also. Do not assume your children are not experiencing
pain because they do not communicate it. Try to see that
they have an opportunity to talk with someone about
their feelings, even if it isn't you. An understanding
school counselor might be able to help.

POSTADOLESCENTS

Postadolescents, aged eighteen to twenty-two, may find
their father's death hard to take not only because of
their own loss but because they may feel that the death
will interfere with their plans for autonomy or going to
school. They may feel they will have to get jobs instead
to help support you. You may want children of this age
to stay home and live with you instead of going off to college. They may feel that lack of funds will keep them
home. The problem becomes more difficult when you
and they do not sit down to discuss what is possible,
both for them and for you. If it is at all possible, you
should try to allow your children to continue with their
plans for independence, even though, in your vulner-

ability, you would like them to continue to need you at least for a while. The reality of another loss, the loss of your child to his or her own adult life, is one you may not want to face. However, if you prevent your children from finding their own paths in life at this point, they may never make the break that is so necessary for young adults. If financial problems mean that the child cannot go on in school, look into scholarships, grants, or loans. But help your child make the break so that you do not develop unhealthy bonds with him or her that will be more difficult to break later.

DATING

The widow with children may find herself in a difficult situation. She may wish to date again, for her own social needs, but may be concerned about the effect on her children. Many widows have avoided dating, using their need to be good parents and their children's need for their full attention as reasons.

When a widow feels either guilty or fearful about dating, she may unconsciously make her innocent children responsible for her own wish to avoid dealing with men. She does not date because "the children don't approve." This is self-defeating in two ways: (1) the children feel a great responsibility for you, and your sacrifice is seen as being their fault; and (2) the children will eventually leave home, or at least should when they are old enough, and then your sacrifice leaves you doubly alone.

When you do decide to date, your younger children may ask the man, often embarrassing both him and you, "Will you be our new daddy?" Younger children have overly high hopes, since they are not aware of what dating and marriage involve. They want a replacement for their father. They need to be told that you are not planning to marry anyone unless you know him very well and unless you and the man decide that you care about each other enough. If you have hidden hopes of remarriage, it is important that you look at your own feelings and are clear about them so that your children understand and accept your explanation.

Older children may react differently to your dating. They may be jealous of any man who comes into the house. One woman was worried because her eleven-year-old was sullen and refused even to speak to her dates. Children of this age miss their father. They probably remember him well enough to feel they don't want some other man to take his place. It is up to you to let preadolescents know that you have a life of your own to lead even though no one can ever exactly replace their dad. Adolescents may either resent your dating or react by helping you to get ready for your first date as if you were a teenager, too.

In this chapter, I have tried to touch on some of the behavior most often exhibited by children after the death of their father. The one question I have been asked most often by widows is, "How can I make up to my child for the death of his father?" My answer is that you can't. You can never make up for the loss the child has suffered. No matter how you may try to be both mother and father, you are only one person and can give only so much to your child. The child will have some needs that you cannot fill. The sooner you realize this and stop feeling guilty about the loss your children have suffered, the sooner you will be able to offer more of yourself to them. Children can be a joy once you stop being "supermom." They are one part of yourself and your husband that you have not lost.

SUGGESTED READINGS

Fazzler, Joan. *My Grandpa Died Today.* New York: Human Sciences Press, 1971. (Deals with the problems of children four to eight.)

Grollman, Earl A. *Talking About Death: A Dialogue Between Parent and Child with Parent's Guide and Recommended Resources.* New edition. Boston: Beacon Press, 1976.

Lorenzo, Carol L. *Mama's Ghosts.* New York: Harper & Row, Publishers, 1978. (Deals with the problems of children ten or older.)

Kantrowitz, Mildred. *When Violet Died.* New York: Parents' Magazine Press, 1973.

Skin, Sara B. *About Dying: An Open Family Book for Parents and Children Together.* New York: Walker & Company, 1972.

Stolz, Mary. *The Edge of Next Year.* New York: Harper & Row, Publishers, 1974. (Deals with the problems of children twelve or older.)

Zolotow, Charlotte. *My Grandson Lew.* New York: Harper & Row, Publishers, 1974.

Chapter 10

Household Hints Heloise Never Gave You

Living alone is rough. Cooking for one is a drag. Cleaning—for whom? Widows with younger children may face living alone later, when the children leave. But the aloneness has to be faced, sooner or later. In previous chapters, I have discussed your emotional needs. In this chapter, I'd like to tell you about some of the practical ways in which many widows have coped with the problems of living alone.

HOME SECURITY

It is important to feel secure in your surroundings. Many women who live alone develop support systems. One woman set up a signal system with her next-door neighbor. When either of them left the house in her car, she honked a code, "I'm leaving." When she returned, she honked an "I'm back" signal. This code made both neighbors feel more secure.

Many widows who do not have family nearby have developed a system whereby a designated person telephones them daily at a particular time to make sure they are all right. In some cities, "telephone reassurance" is offered by social service groups. If the widow doesn't answer, the designated person will call a neighbor or family member, and someone will check to make sure the woman is all right. Older people often find this system particularly useful, but anyone living alone can have an accident. The buddy system is a safeguard against lying unconscious for days in your house or apartment.

Security can be a problem for widows. Many tell me they have put more locks on their doors. Others say they do not open the door to strangers or that they keep a chain latch on while opening the door. Precautions are probably wise.

Some women have found that a large dog can be a companion as well as a protector. Moreover, a dog is a living creature who needs its owner. It is important not to make the pet into a substitute husband by putting all your energies into the animal, but a warm, furry friend can add to your existence.

Another suggestion to offer a sense of security is to install a garage-door opener that you can operate from your car. This relieves you of the need, on a dark night, to get out of your car before you are safely inside your garage.

Of course, the area around your house should remain well lighted in the evenings.

WAKING UP

One of the hardest things for the newly widowed is to get up in the morning. Unless you have a job to go to, and even if you do, the feeling of "What's it worth?" gets in the way of really moving. Waking up to pleasant music on your clock radio is one suggestion.

A friend can be a help when you find yourself too depressed to get up in the morning. Ask your friend, preferably also widowed so as to be more understanding, to call you every morning about a half hour before you have to get up. The human contact, the awareness that someone cares, and the routine of knowing you will be called will all help. The friend can keep talking until you feel able to face the day. Sooner or later you will find yourself feeling better without even realizing it.

COMING HOME

Coming home to an empty house can be devastating. Although the aloneness can't be changed, there is no reason to punish yourself with silence and darkness as well.

One widow told me she solved the problem with an automatic timer. She set the timer to turn on the lights in the living room twenty minutes before she was home. She came home to a lighted house and had a much more relaxed feeling about entering her door. Timers can also be used to turn on the radio or TV. They can be attached to any appliance and set for any time you desire.

COOKING AND EATING

Cooking for one can be a chore or a challenge, depending on how you see it. When you were married, you often set special tables for your husband and yourself. Ask yourself, "Why can't I set the table in a festive mood for myself once in a while?" One of the most important things a person can do is to give to himself or herself. So often in our lives, we give to others, but how often do we give to ourselves? A flower at the table, a well-set table, food that you like to eat, music while eating. You may not feel ready to do this during the first few months after you are widowed, but if it sounds like something you can consider now, try it. Remember, you need not feel guilty because you are alive.

Food has a number of meanings for different people, and its emotional meanings are much more involved than many people recognize. One widow who could not sit down to eat kept pacing back and forth throughout the house, snacking as she walked. She ate crazy things. Realizing she was jeopardizing her health, she invited herself to a friend's for dinner, saying, "Please let me eat with you, or I will go crazy." For more than a year, until she felt able to face eating alone, she ate with this friend—sharing food costs, of course. Realizing that your feelings are natural, and pampering yourself for a while, can mean a better recovery for you after a period of time.

Other suggestions about eating alone include eating at a table in front of the TV, with an actor or reporter as your dinner guest; propping up an absorbing book; doing crossword puzzles; or sitting in the seat your husband used so you do not look at his empty chair. Try to eat well-balanced meals. Your health is at a critical point now. The physical demands on you have been enormous —dealing with a funeral, financial crises, and so forth. Take care of yourself. Even though you have lost your spouse, you still have yourself to think about.

HOME APPLIANCES

Many home appliances, though not specifically designed for the purpose, can make eating alone easier. These include microwave ovens, which will cook a meal in a few minutes; toaster-ovens; blenders; coffee makers that brew two to three cups of coffee at a time; plug-in water warmers (so you don't leave the stove on and burn pots by cooking water too long); and plastic bags that allow you to freeze leftover food and reheat the bags when you want a quick meal.

ENTERTAINING ALONE

When you have been used to entertaining as part of a couple, beginning to have people over as a single person can become something to put off. It is a big step forward to feel that you can entertain without your husband. The idea of cooking a large dinner may not appeal to you. There is no rule that says you must have people over for dinner. How about starting by inviting some folks for dessert and coffee? Or ask each friend to bring a cooked dish and have a potluck dinner. You will not have to do all the work, and friends will be able to share their culinary arts. Maybe a course in French or Chinese cooking will offer you new ideas and even find you new friends.

You may feel it is impossible to tend to the drinks, cook, serve, and be a good hostess, too. You can ask a friend to help with the drinks or have your guests help themselves. You can prepare as much as possible early, before guests arrive, so your time in the kitchen is cut down. You do not have to have formal dinners, even if they may have been in fashion when you were part of a couple. Be inventive and and serve informally. Many women's magazines offer recipes that you may want to try out on friends.

The key to entertaining alone is knowing your weaknesses and anxieties and working around them so that you can feel comfortable in your new role and begin to enjoy entertaining again.

REARRANGING YOUR HOME

One of the problems often mentioned is how to stay in the same house you shared while married, when everything there reminds you of your husband.

One suggestion is to rearrange the furniture. Some people remove their husband's favorite chair; others find that by taking over the chair and sitting in it themselves, they do not have to face the empty chair and even gain some sense of security.

Another suggestion is to recover the furniture in a pattern you enjoy so that the house begins to take on more of your own character.

Many people have found it helpful to move out of the

bedroom they shared with their spouse into a different room. Another suggestion is to stay in the same bedroom but sleep on the side of the bed that your spouse used to occupy. Until one widow found this answer, she would reach over during the night and expect to find her husband there. Since she now sleeps where he did, this pattern has been broken, and she has less pain from the unfulfilled expectation.

Other suggestions about sleeping arrangements include sleeping with pillows arranged on the other side of the bed. One woman found she slept best on the couch, where its back cuddled her back.

HOME AND AUTO REPAIRS

Home and auto repairs are two areas in which many women feel basically incompetent. Although some people suggest taking courses in these subjects, this is impractical for many women, especially if they are working. Other women do not choose to learn to do these things for themselves.

If you do not "do it yourself," you need to find good and trustworthy help. In many communities, retired men will gladly do home repairs at reasonable prices. Check with your senior center or an information and referral service. In one town, a local hardware store kept a file of people who wanted to do handyman jobs. Teenagers will also do odd jobs for spending money. Friends and neighbors may know someone who is trustworthy and handy. They may also know of a reputable garage.

HUSBAND'S BELONGINGS

What to do with your husband's clothing? One woman told me, "I got rid of his clothes and all his things right away. I didn't want to be reminded of him at all. I thought this was best, and I haven't regretted it."

Another widow, however, stated, "It's been three years, and though I have gotten rid of some stuff, I can't seem to give away his favorite robe. Sometimes, when I feel low, I put it on and it seems to comfort me."

When a person close to you dies, it is natural to want to remember him. For some people, tangible reminders are useful. For others, they cause too much pain—memories are enough. Like most other decisions you make when you are widowed, your decision in regard to your husband's belongings must be right for you. One of the worst ways of solving the problem is to allow children or other relatives to clean out the closet without consulting you. This is the kind of thing that prolongs grief. You should decide when and how your husband's clothes and possessions will be disposed of. If you don't want to be involved, okay. But it should be your decision.

The giving up of possessions that belonged to the deceased can be a time when grief work is accomplished. A caring friend or relative, willing to be with the widow, will allow her to cry when she remembers how Bill used to enjoy a particular tie or when she remembers the Christmas when she gave him that plaid shirt. By remembering, by giving her emotions room, the widow is doing the grief work so necessary to the resolution of her feelings of loss and the gaining of a new perspective.

Basically, to recover from widowhood, you have to change habits that you developed with your husband to habits that fit you now. This may mean that the house does not get the same attention it did because other things are more important to you. Your patterns may be different. They have to be right for you.

The disorganization you feel stems in part from the lack of defined habits that work for you now that you are widowed. By redefining what you do in terms of your needs now, you will in time develop a way of functioning that works for you in the present and that will help you toward a more self-reliant future.

SUGGESTED READINGS

Action for Independent Maturity. *AIM's Guide to Single Living*. Washington, D.C.: Action for Independent Maturity, 1977. (Available for 20¢ from AIM, 1909 K St. NW, Washington, D.C. 20049.)

Liles, Marcia D., and Liles, Robert M. *Good Housekeeping Guide to Fixing Things Around the House*. New York: Pocket Books, 1976.

Parker, Elinor. *Cooking for One*. 5th rev. ed. New York: Thomas Y. Crowell Company, Inc., 1976.

Chapter 11

Should I or Shouldn't I?

What does a woman do about her sexual impulses after her husband dies? What about her need to be touched, to be held, to have a man who cares about her? Does she fall in love again? Does she adjust to the new morality? These are all questions to which most married women give little thought. But for the woman who is widowed they are questions that must be dealt with and resolved.

Age can affect your feelings about love, intimacy, and sexuality. If you are older and were raised with the idea that love and sex are part and parcel of marriage and not acceptable outside of marriage, you will have different expectations for yourself and others as you wrestle with your emotions than you will if you are younger or more accepting of the newer view, based on recent research into human sexuality, that sexual urges require expression.

The questions are complex, and each person must find her own answer. But the process may become easier if we share some of the problems that many widows struggle with.

108

SEXUAL URGES

In doing research on this topic, I learned that some widows find themselves wanting men sexually soon after their husbands die. This is true of women who had good sexual relations with their husbands as well as those whose relations were less satisfying. In a widows' discussion group, one woman said, almost guiltily, "My sexual feelings were greatly intensified after my husband's death. I felt like jumping into bed with the first man I saw." What surprised her was that other women in the group owned up to similar feelings, which they did not understand and of which they felt ashamed. In airing their feelings, they realized that their heightened ardor was not crazy or strange.

The question of why sexual urges should be so strong was discussed, and several ideas emerged. One woman missed the regularity of sexual intercourse she had enjoyed during marriage. Another woman, whose husband had been too ill for several months to have intercourse with her, felt that her need arose from the deprivation she had experienced. Still another woman felt rejected by her husband's death, in a way she couldn't explain, and needed to prove that she was still sexually attractive.

An older widow, in her sixties, asked how other older widows handled their sexual urges. Because sex has been a taboo topic and because older women have traditionally grown up with strict views about sex, especially unmarried sex, many older women felt hesitant about discussing their feelings within the group.

Unlike the younger women, one older woman who had been widowed four years had not dated at all, even though she had recovered in other ways. She was frightened of what would be expected of her and still was wed to the memory of her husband. To her, dating would have meant defiling his memory. Another older widow had not dated after her husband died because, as she explained, "He knew my body and was not put off by my wrinkles. Another man would not find me attractive. So I don't even try."

What emerged most distinctly from discussions about sexual urges is that the need is as much for physical contact, touching and being cared about, as for the physical release that sex itself brings. Your husband gave you physical caring, a sense of belonging, and the feeling that your body was attractive to him. His touching you, either in a quick hello or good-bye kiss or in the passions of your bed, is lost after his death. Your need for his touch and physical caress can translate itself into sexual intensity. Recognizing this as a natural reaction may alleviate some of your guilt over having such feelings and allow you to handle the feelings in a positive way.

Another reaction, as frequent as having intense sexual desires, is having no sexual desire at all during the first year of widowhood and often for two or three years after. It is as though the widow has buried her sexuality along with her husband. When questioned about this, most women felt it would be disloyal to their husbands to have sex with another man.

These widows often felt that other men wanted only sex. They often talked of sexual advances made by neighbors, married friends, and single men. One woman commented, "Men I have known for a long time and with whom I used to joke easily seem to have problems with me now. There are sexual overtones to the jokes that used to be just jokes." She was worried about how to deal with this intensified sexual interest in her. I suggested that she had assumed a different role, one with which her male friends were uncomfortable. She was safe before, married and untouchable. Now she is alone. Some men now see her as available and fair game. I suggested that, if she had the courage, she should call them on it. She might say, "I really enjoy our friendship, but a strange quality has crept into it. I am the same person I was when I was married to George, yet I am more vulnerable now. And I would appreciate it if you respect me as you did when George was alive." Although the men may deny that they meant anything by their remarks, your frankness may cause the relationship to take on a more relaxed, less sexually tinged tone.

FEELING UGLY

Some women have indicated that they feel ugly now that their husbands are dead. The older woman quoted above was one example. But younger widows also often feel that they have lost their beauty. One woman told me that she was sitting near the pool in her apartment complex a few months after her husband died and a young man approached her and said hello. She looked up, got up, and fled to her apartment. "I felt so ugly, I didn't understand how he could even look at me."

Since our view of ourselves often depends on how others see us, we need reinforcement from those we trust. Your husband reinforced your feeling that you are pretty by complimenting you on a new outfit, perfume, a new hairstyle. Since he is no longer here to provide that reinforcement, you may feel that you don't count. It is important for you to find ways to enhance your feelings of self-worth so that you do not see yourself only through the eyes of others.

This may take some time and effort, but it is vital that you do not allow feelings of ugliness to dominate your existence. Find out what looks good on you and wear it. Counter the "blahs" by taking extra care of your face and figure so that you provide your *own* reinforcement each time you look in the mirror. Force yourself to go out each day, looking your best. Although this is important in terms of how you appear to others, especially men, it is more important that *you* begin to see yourself as pleasant-looking again.

DATING AND SEXUALITY

Once you have begun to see yourself as attractive again, you may wonder how to find male companionship without being obvious. Bernadine Kreis, a sensitive widow, in her book *To Love Again: An Answer to Loneliness*, describes, from her own experiences, how she developed a philosophy regarding where to go to find that special person: "Little children know the answer. They eagerly embrace what they enjoy whether it be a toy or a person. They are spontaneous, curious and honest. . . . As we grow . . . we tend to overadjust . . . and the child goes deep within us, so deep that we lose the talent for being spontaneous, curious and honest."

She suggests that luck, in the form of chance encounters, can be a way to meet people. She feels that you don't have to be serious about every date. Think of each date as an adventure and bring to it enthusiasm and friendliness: "There's only one way to find love and that's by meeting people—a process that can be painful and frightening but also a stimulating and rewarding adventure."

By being active and keeping busy with projects you enjoy, you will exude interestedness and involvement, which will attract friends—both men and women. Of course, the next problem becomes what to do with the men who are attracted to you.

A younger widow asked me what to do about a man she was dating. "I have been widowed nine months and now have met a nice man with whom I go out. He would like to go to bed with me, but I feel anxious about it. I somehow feel I would be betraying my husband. What do you think?" I explained to her, and would say to you, that you have to make the decision that fits you best, both emotionally and in terms of your own values. One thing to recognize, sooner or later, is that you are no longer married to your husband. He is dead. Another important thing to realize is that, after only nine months, you are probably still too newly widowed to become emotionally involved with someone else. You might need affection, but you are not ready for a new love. Therefore the answer is three-pronged:

First, try not to become emotionally involved with anyone until you feel you are recovering from your grief and can see the person as an individual.

Second, if you feel that you want to, do relieve your physical needs. The idea of betraying your husband assumes that he is still alive and will walk in on you. Once you have said good-bye and let go of your husband, you will no longer feel that it is betrayal to be attracted to another man.

Third, do not feel you have to go to bed with anyone, unless you want to and feel ready to.

Another woman, widowed about eighteen months, was afraid of becoming emotionally involved with a man she was seeing. She felt that if they were married and he died, she wouldn't be able to bear it. The woman who has had a satisfying marital relationship may very well feel lost and abandoned when her husband dies. She may want to protect herself from ever feeling again the loss she felt after her spouse died. This invisible shield of self-protection is her way of making sure she never goes through all the pain again. One widow expressed the attitude I feel each widow needs to develop when she said, "When you are a caring person and you get involved with people, you do take your chances. But to experience pain is better than to experience nothing." What she said so eloquently is that a protective shield dulls your sensitivity and your living of life and ultimately does you a disservice.

Dating again, after being married for a number of years, is a totally new experience. You have to recognize that the rules changed while you were married. There is a much freer attitude toward dating and sex. Many women, older and younger, are beginning to feel that they have a right to enjoy sexuality.

Masters and Johnson, Hite, and many others who have researched the topic of human sexuality agree that women have the right to enjoy sex. This new attitude toward sex is based on physical findings—women are sexual creatures, as are men, and need to express their sexual needs. Thus, if a woman chooses to, she can have a sexual relationship with a man without having a strong emotional involvement. A woman can also satisfy herself sexually by using a vibrator or by masturbating. Ultimately, the individual must make her own decision about what she does with her body.

The most important things to remember when you are concerned about your sexuality are these:

First, you are no longer married. As a single woman, you have the right to decide for yourself what to do with your life in all areas.

Second, your own values are the most important.

Third, you are not alone in your concern about sexuality. Try to discuss your feelings with other single people—it may help to put your feelings into perspective.

One widow, who had had only one sexual relationship in her life, with her husband, was a sexually attractive woman with a healthy interest in sex. However, it took her seven years after her husband died to feel comfortable having sexual relations with another man, though she did relieve her tensions by masturbating. She decided, after the affair, that she needed more than just sex. What is most important in this situation is that it is her body and she has the right to do what she feels is best for her.

AFFAIRS

Defined as a relationship that is not entered into with the idea that it is necessarily permanent or binding, an affair can be either a trauma or a new and good experience for a widow, depending on how well she feels the affair meets her needs. An affair will not work for the woman who wants a long-term, committed, one-to-one relationship. On the other hand, one woman I interviewed has had several affairs since she was widowed. She does not expect total commitment from any man she is involved with, yet she has given much to and received much from each affair. Since she is able to handle these relationships, it seems an excellent way for her to relieve sexual tension, enjoy male companionship, and meet her need for closeness and physical touching. This woman is somewhat independent and does not expect an affair to meet all her needs. She is not asking for a husband and accepts the limitations of the affair.

Some women who have affairs, especially with married men, do not accept the limitations of an affair. Lynn Caine, in her book *Lifelines*, has an excellent chapter on falling in love again, in which she discusses affairs with married men. She makes the cogent observation that "one does not become engaged to a married man. . . . I've seen too many women postpone their lives, living in the hope that one day this married man would marry them."

A relationship with a married man cannot offer total fulfillment because of the nature of the man's other commitments. The widow who needs her self-esteem enhanced will not find such an affair rewarding. She can never get enough of the man who has other obligations. She should be forewarned that a married man seldom leaves his wife and family, no matter how rotten he says his life is.

REMARRIAGE

You need to be cautious about remarriage. Often loneliness can lead to remarriage, with negative consequences. Certainly, remarriage should not be considered until you feel you have said good-bye to your dead spouse. A new husband should not be a replacement for your dead husband but should be considered as an individual in his own right.

There are many things to consider when you think of remarriage. One of the most important is children. The younger widow often asks, "Do I marry someone when my children are younger, or do I try to raise them myself because no one can take their father's place?" It used to be quite common for the widow to remain a widow, at least until her children were grown. She had a sense of pride and fulfillment in caring for her children without a stepfather. This is less true of today's widow.

Children's response to the possibility of a new father may deter a widow from even thinking about remarriage. This is unfortunate, since a woman's happiness may be postponed or completely destroyed if she allows her children to dominate her. On the other hand, remarriage solely for the sake of giving the children a male figure to identify with can also be disastrous. Although children should be consulted, they should not have the final say in your decision to remarry.

Adult children often find it hard to accept their mother's need for male companionship, her sexuality, and her interest in remarriage. They don't realize that for the older widow, the possibilities for relationships with men of similar age diminish. More than half the women over sixty-five are widowed; only one out of seven older men are widowed.

Because of your adult children's view of you as an asexual creature, they may frown on any remarriage plans you share with them. It is important to realize that they are truly concerned about you. They may be concerned about the man's motives and worried about your future safety. However, if you feel the relationship you have with a man is worthwhile, and you want to marry, ask your children to recognize your needs and accept them as valid. If you do not get their approval, but the relationship seems important enough to you, you may be in conflict. I would urge you, after considering all the pros and cons of remarriage, to realize that you have too few precious years left to allow others to determine what is best for you. Your children must recognize that you are an adult with many years of good sense behind you. This assumes, of course, that you are over the major part of your grief and have based the decision to remarry on the realities of the present, not on memories of the past.

Other factors to consider in remarriage include dissimilar backgrounds, entrenched habits, old friends of each of the partners, and differences that can become cause for estrangement. The person you want to marry has a background, habits, and values that he has lived with for a long time. You will not be able to change those patterns; you need to learn to live with them. Viewing this as an adventure and challenge will enhance the marriage. Knowing someone well enough before you marry is important, to avoid being shocked afterward by behavior you did not anticipate.

When a widow marries too soon, divorce is often the result. The new husband does not live up to the deceased husband's image. In truth, the new widow does not have the emotional stability to make a sound decision about remarriage.

Once married, you will have to clear the ghosts out of your closets. You and your husband, especially if he is widowed or divorced, will have expectations based on your first marriages that may not be appropriate to the new situation. You will have to deal with your partner as a new and different lover if you want your marriage to be fulfilling in its own right.

A widow is very vulnerable. She needs time and the stability that comes with getting herself together before she becomes involved in any relationship with the expectation that it will be a fulfilling give-and-take situation. Most relationships she enters into before she has recovered will be based on her needfulness, her lack of faith in herself, and her seeking the lost love she feels she has been deprived of.

But once you have said good-bye to your spouse, and see yourself as a whole person again, your options are many and varied in this area as in every other.

SUGGESTED READINGS

Butler, Robert N., and Lewis, Myrna I. *Sex After 60: A Guide for Men and Women for Their Later Years.* New York: Harper & Row, Publishers, 1976.

Caine, Lynn. *Lifelines.* Garden City, N.Y.: Doubleday & Company, Inc., 1978.

Hite, Shere. *The Hite Report.* New York: Dell Publishing Company, Inc., 1977.

Kreis, Bernadine. *To Love Again: An Answer to Loneliness.* New York: The Seabury Press, Inc., 1975.

Masters, William H., and Johnson, Virginia E. *Human Sexual Response.* Boston: Little, Brown and Company, 1966.

Tavris, Carol. "The Sexual Lives of Women over 60." *Ms. Magazine,* June 1977, pp. 62–65.

Chapter 12

I've Become a Person Again

"I knew I was recovering when I started putting mushrooms into the spaghetti sauce. Bob hated mushrooms. I love them!"

Emerging from grief after saying good-bye means different things to different people. One widow told me, proudly but sadly, that her husband would not know her now. She was proud at how much she had grown and sad at the price she had to pay. Yet growth must come unless a woman is stuck, like Queen Victoria was.

Once you accept your grief, your fears, your aloneness —once you say good-bye—then you can say, "Yes, I am alone. He is dead," and go on with your life. This acceptance cannot be forced on you by others. Your own timetable will determine when you are ready to become more than just a widow.

What is this feeling of having hit bottom and starting up again? What is it like to emerge from widowhood to a place where your thoughts and deeds are not all tied to the past, where you have a life in the present and thoughts about the future? Many widows have shared with me their thoughts about their recovery.

"I feel guilty that I am not as involved in thinking

119

about my husband anymore. He is not in my thoughts every minute and that feels good, but I am afraid I will forget him."

"I'm doing things I couldn't do when I was married."

"I will always miss my husband for all those shared experiences that only he and I can remember. Now I remember them myself, smile, and continue with whatever I'm doing."

"I felt I had recovered when I took responsibility for being a person again."

"As long as I thought of myself as a wife and was unable to give that up, I couldn't move on. Once I realized that I was no one's wife but was a person who counted just the same, I began to feel much better about things."

"I feel torn between a tug to be grieving and my own desire to make a new life."

When you begin to emerge from your grief, you discover that your husband is not constantly in your thoughts. You find other things to occupy you. As you begin to invest your surplus physical and psychological energy in persons and activities that offer you emotional support and encouragement, there is a fear of forgetting your husband. You may feel guilty about potentialities that emerged only after his death. You want to go on, and you do. Yet at moments you panic. If you allow yourself to overcome this panic, you become a person again.

Feeling widowed implies that you belong to someone. This is appropriate when you are grieving, working through your feelings about your mate. But once you say good-bye and let go, you are in reality no longer attached. One woman, widowed four years, said, "There is some part of me that rebels against playing the role of widow." She hit on a most vital point. Although the void never quite goes away, you do not have to play the widow's role for the rest of your life.

Getting married again is one option. Many women have explored other options and found them meaningful. Most important is one's definition of oneself. If after a number of years of widowhood, you are still only his widow, there is need for you to assess what it is you are getting out of clinging to this concept of yourself.

In this chapter, let's explore, one by one, some of the options open to you as you begin to live in the present and make plans for your future.

CARING ABOUT YOURSELF

As you emerge from widowhood to personhood, take a good, hard look at your face, your body, your clothes. Now I will ask *you* some questions.

Can you become important enough to yourself to care about yourself? Can you begin to live for yourself? This does not mean that you become a selfish, uncaring individual. It does mean you can give to yourself. If you care about yourself, caring about others comes naturally.

Look at your hair. Treat yourself to an appointment with a hairstylist, especially if you have let yourself go. Try a new hairdo.

Women go on buying sprees when newly widowed or they hold tightly to every penny. Let the pendulum stop in the middle and take a look at your wardrobe. Does it suit you as you see yourself now? Your husband may have liked you in pink. Do you like yourself in pink? If not, what is *your* favorite color? What will make you feel good? Why not treat yourself to some new clothes that fit your present image of yourself?

You may be concerned about money. If this is a problem, try the resale shops. Most cities have stores that sell, on consignment, designer fashions that have been worn only a few times. Shop around. You may be able to find a "Second Chance" store that has the kind of clothes that look good on you.

Look at your body. Are you pleased with it? I personally do not agree that skinny is beautiful. Crash diets hurt more than they help. But keeping your body in good physical condition is important to good health and to your self-concept—which, by the way, is enhanced when your body and your mental image of it match.

If you enjoy routine, exercise and proper eating habits should be no problem. If, on the other hand, you despise repetition, exercise and good eating habits will be more difficult for you to get used to and maintain. Community programs can help you. Try a YWCA or community recreation program of exercise or a yoga or swim class. When you exercise with others, it doesn't seem like such a chore. I have had positive personal experience with yoga as a form of exercise that enhances body image and control.

Look at your eating habits. You may find that you have been eating to fill up your loneliness. Instead of reaching for the refrigerator door, reach for the phone. Call a friend and talk until the loneliness has been allayed. If you have stopped eating, find a friend to share meals with so that you eat regularly.

Go slowly. You don't need to change overnight. You will find yourself backsliding from time to time, but as long as you keep heading in the right direction, up from widowhood, you will be amazed at how well you will feel, in time.

FRIENDSHIPS

Widows often feel left out. They speak of feeling like fifth wheels because friends who are couples do not include them in their social arrangements. A person (I shall no longer use the term *widow* in order to underline the basic premise of this chapter) can choose to sit home, feeling left out. She can, on the other hand, begin to develop friendships of her own on the basis of her current interests and needs.

After you have assessed what these are, you may begin by taking classes, going to work, or doing volunteer work. You will meet other women to talk to, to enjoy lunch with, to go bowling with, or to go with to the theater or symphony. You may meet men whom you want to get to know.

The first step is asking. Ask an interesting woman or man whom you see in class or at work if she or he would like to have coffee with you. Some women will not ask for fear they will be rejected. Think about that for a moment. What is the worst thing that will happen to you if you are rejected? Confronting your fears and finding out what they mean to you can be revealing. Confronted fears often disappear. One thing we usually forget is that most other people want to reach out just as much as we do. They are just as shy or unwilling to take a risk. You have an edge. You have lived through the worst possible rejection—the death of your spouse. Anything you encounter now is child's play compared to that.

Once you have taken the first step, seeking friends, you will need to cultivate friendships with persons whose company you enjoy, who offer you stimulating conversation, activities to share, and a sense of worth. You will want to avoid people who see you only as a "poor widow"; this does not help you to see yourself as an individual.

Being assertive by inviting people to your home and not waiting to be invited, trying new activities and not feeling that you can't because they don't fit your husband's image of you, and being adventurous rather than withdrawn can result in rewarding new friendships.

WORK

You may have been a homemaker during your marriage, but now you have to go to work. Or you may choose to start building a career. The job market is tight. Younger women with up-to-date skills are in demand. The challenge is great. You need to think creatively to overcome the barriers you will encounter.

Brush up on any skills you had before you were married. Many women have also, during marriage, acquired skills of which they are unaware but do not interpret their daily lives in terms of the job market. Volunteer experience, home management skills, and help you gave your husband with his business can all be parlayed into a job if you view them creatively.

Talk to people about jobs wherever and whenever you can. You never know when an opportunity may arise. It may be necessary to submit a resume before you are considered for a job. A resume is a catalog of your job qualifications and should state, attractively and systematically, who you are, what you know, what you have done, what kind of work you want, and why you should be hired. Using the resume is standard practice, especially in professional, scientific, executive, and managerial positions. Preparing one will help you organize your assets and start you thinking about your qualifications. By assembling the facts about yourself beforehand, you will avoid useless interviews and build your confidence for the interviews you will need to have. There are a number of books, mentioned in Suggested Readings at the end of this chapter, that will give you more pointers on resumes.

One of the most important aspects of job hunting is the job interview. If you have a positive attitude about yourself and your abilities, you will exude this during interviews. If you see yourself as just a housewife, you will come across that way to a prospective employer. Consider job interviews as practice. Do not expect to get the first or even the second job for which you apply.

When you have an interview scheduled, these pointers may help you put your best foot forward:

1. Learn about your employer. Don't hesitate to ask questions about the firm or the specific job.
2. Be on time, or even five to ten minutes early.

3. Do not go to an interview "dragged out." Try to be alert and rested for an interview.
4. Dress appropriately.
5. Go alone.
6. Be confident. Remember, you have something to offer the company.
7. Think before you answer questions, and listen carefully.
8. Don't look for sympathy. The employer is interested only in how well you fit the position, not in your personal problems.
9. Don't downgrade yourself. Accentuate the positive.

If you do not get the job for which you apply, ask the interviewer what you lacked in terms of what he or she was looking for so you can learn from each interview. You will begin to find your confidence increasing if you approach interviews in this way instead of expecting too much from each one.

I have often heard the adage "You only get a job when when you already have one." Since getting a job when you are unemployed seems much more difficult, it may be wise to take a less elegant job while hunting for a better one. Do not feel tied to any job. If a better job comes along and you want it, take it.

Social Security may give the woman with younger children a respite from the need to find work immediately. Remember, however, that Social Security for children stops when they are eighteen, or twenty-two if they are full-time students, and it stops for you when they are eighteen and does not start again until you are sixty. Therefore, while you are still receiving Social Security for your children, think about what kind of job you will want when they are on their own. You really have an edge over the woman who is forced to go to work without preparation. You have time to take courses, brush up on skills, or perhaps find a part-time job that can lead to full-time employment when you need it.

One woman with younger children always wanted to be a photographer. She takes portraits, working from her home. She is developing a thriving business. Look at your own talents and skills and decide how to make them work for you.

Social Security is minimal or nonexistent for many widows with young children whose husbands were employed in marginal or exempt jobs. In these situations, finding a job becomes necessary, but it also becomes more difficult, and the difficulty is compounded by the need to find adequate care for the children. A competent sitter who comes to your house or apartment may cost more than you can afford. Taking the children to the sitter or to a day-care center means transporting them, a major undertaking at seven each morning and at six each evening of every working day.

Day-care centers exist in most cities, usually for children of two and older. Some centers for infants also exist in various cities. The Department of Human Resources usually handles the licensing of day-care centers and homes and will send you a list of licensed facilities upon request. It is important to visit the centers personally to see what kind of care your child will receive. Beware of any center that seems too rigid. Children in care centers all day need warmth, attention, and stimulation and should be allowed some freedom and creative activity in their "home away from home." If you enroll your child and find, after a reasonable length of time, that the child really doesn't like the situation, look into the complaints. Children are very perceptive and can usually be trusted to express their feelings of contentment or frustration.

If you were working when you husband died, that job can be nourishing to you now. Many women have felt that work was their salvation after their husbands died. But now that you are redefining your opportunities, you may want to take a good hard look at your job and decide whether it still meets your needs. If it does not, you may want to assess what you want out of your work and begin to develop strategies for change.

One magazine I would recommend is *Working Woman*. It contains articles helpful to the woman who is working and the woman who wants to change her occupation.

TRAINING AND CAREER COUNSELING

Displaced homemakers is a term used to define women (or men) whose major jobs as homemakers have been disrupted by the divorce, death, or abandonment of their spouses.

A number of states have passed Displaced Homemakers' bills, which call for setting up centers to help these people find work through job training, assertiveness training, and on-the-job training. A federal Displaced Homemakers' bill is also pending in Congress. The Displaced Homemakers' Network, housed at the Business and Professional Women's Foundation, 2012 Massachusetts Avenue NW, Washington, D.C. 20036, telephone (202) 293–1200, can let you know the current status of this bill as well as give you the addresses of centers already functioning in states that have passed Displaced Homemakers' bills.

Many women, those who are trying to decide whether to return to school or to work as well as those reentering the job market, find career-counseling services helpful. Career counseling is a burgeoning field, and many colleges and universities have career-counseling courses or centers. Rather than finding you a specific job, a career counselor can help you make decisions about what you want to do and teach you how to make contacts, write a good resume, and conduct yourself in a job interview. Moreover, counseling will give you support, especially if you feel that you have nothing to offer in the job market.

Career-counseling courses usually take from five to ten sessions. They are structured situations in which you learn to have more confidence in the skills you have and receive guidance so that you can look for work more effectively. Courses are provided by women's centers, YWCAs, and community colleges. A center that offers a variety of programs and such supportive services as lectures, films, an in-house career library, and a follow-up system is best. Catalyst, a career-counseling agency (14 East Sixtieth Street, New York, N.Y. 10022) has a list of career-counseling and placement services that meet its standards of quality.

EDUCATION

If you have a job and the work is boring, consider taking classes at night. Many women find that returning to college affords them the opportunity for better-paying, more interesting positions. If you are financially able to support yourself at present (through Social Security or veterans' benefits, for example) but want to prepare for the future, returning to school may offer you that opportunity. Most universities and colleges are aware of the needs of older women who want to return to school and are integrating these mature students into their student population and offering support and encouragement to them.

Education as a lifelong process keeps the mind active and the spirit young. Many persons have found that returning to school has added spark and vitality to their lives. Many colleges offer continuing education courses on practical as well as academic subjects. Tuition is minimal at community colleges, and scholarships may be available. School is no longer only for the young or the wealthy.

SUPPORT SYSTEMS

"Going it alone" is very tough. The women's centers mentioned previously offer many kinds of support to the woman alone who is trying to come out of herself. Through the women's movement, women's organizations are developing sisterhood and breaking down the age barriers among women.

The local chapters of the National Organization for Women (425 Thirteenth Street NW, Washington, D.C. 20008) offer women a common meeting ground and a voice for their concerns. There are other groups that give a woman a sense of belonging. Some of these are Business and Professional Women (2012 Massachusetts Avenue NW, Washington, D.C. 20008), American Association of University Women (2401 Virginia Avenue NW, Washington, D.C. 20037), and Women's Action Alliance (370 Lexington Avenue, New York, N.Y. 10017). Write to these groups to find out about their activities nationally and in your community.

VOLUNTEER WORK

Many women who do not have to go to work to earn a living find volunteer work rewarding. The opportunities are almost endless, and the need for volunteers is great. If you want to do volunteer work, find the work that interests you most. Shop around for the volunteer work that suits you; do not feel obliged to take on any task offered. The work you choose should be meaningful and fulfilling.

You may be interested in one of the many museums that offer courses to individuals who want to become docents. One woman I interviewed is interested in Asian culture; she undertook voluntary work as a docent at a museum that specializes in Asian art.

Another interesting opportunity for volunteers is in

hospitals, working with young children. The children's need for affection and care can give you a chance to share with them some of the affection that you have not been able to express since your husband's death. VISTA, Foster Grandparents, the Retired Senior Volunteer Program (RSVP), and Meals on Wheels are some other opportunities.

Consider volunteering for one of the programs that reach out to the newly widowed. You have weathered your widowhood. Perhaps you can pass along to others some of what you learned through your experience. NRTA–AARP Widowed Persons Service (1909 K Street NW, Washington, D.C. 20049) has a directory of programs in your area for the widowed of all ages.

LEISURE

Close your eyes for a moment, relax, take some deep breaths, and think about what you have always wanted to do but for one reason or another—marriage, children, shyness, lack of funds—you have not done. Now that you can enjoy yourself and do whatever you choose, what would you do?

When I use this exercise with groups of women of all ages, creative and fun answers emerge. A woman in one group always wanted to act. Another woman enjoyed play-reading. The two got together and auditioned for a local little-theater production. A third had always wanted to fly a kite but felt foolish. The other group members encouraged her to "go fly a kite."

My former secretary enjoys folk dancing. She was not able to dance as much as she liked when she was younger because of family responsibilities. She now dances two or three nights a week, has a closetful of ethnic costumes, and is immersed in the joy of dancing. She still feels sad when she remembers her husband, but she knows that this sadness is part of her life. She told me, "At first it was frightening and overwhelming to have freedom. But now it is wonderful to be able to come and go as I choose."

Find places to go to to engage in leisure activities and to do things that are creative, fun, and personally rewarding. Your YWCA offers classes, swimming groups, and usually baby-sitting for the woman with small children. The Y is a friendly place and has been serving the single woman for many, many years.

Your church or synagogue may or may not offer activities for single persons. If its activities are geared toward two-parent families and couples, talk to your priest, minister, or rabbi about developing groups and programs that take into account the special situation of people like yourself. You may find yourself talked into starting such a group. If you are a good organizer, you may find the task rewarding in itself.

Parents Without Partners (PWP) offers women with children opportunities for activities with their children and with other single parents. Some widows who are still quite vulnerable have found the attitude in PWP too social. I suggest you join only when you feel capable of handling yourself emotionally so that you do not feel overwhelmed by male members of the group. PWP offers support to the parent who is single, whether by divorce or death, and has been an important force nationally in having the needs of the single parent recognized. In some PWP chapters, there are groups for the widowed, since there is recognition of the widowed parent's different social and practical problems. To find out where the nearest PWP chapter is, write Parents Without Partners, International Headquarters, 7910 Woodmont Avenue, Bethesda, Maryland 20014.

I have mentioned programs and groups for the widowed throughout this book. As you emerge from grief, these programs may offer you opportunities for voluntary involvement. If there is no local program to help the new widow, you may want to spearhead its development. NRTA–AARP Widowed Persons Service

(WPS) offers guidelines and support in setting up out-reach programs for the widowed. Social groups for the widowed also exist. Write WPS for information about programs near you.

There are senior centers for the older woman in almost every community. Usually for persons over sixty, these centers offer a variety of courses, activities, excursions, and, sometimes, meals. Another possibility for leisure activity, as well as for rewarding community involvement, is to join the American Association of Retired Persons (AARP). Open to persons over fifty-five, AARP offers travel charters, discounts on drugs, an informative magazine, and over three thousand local chapters that have monthly activities and programs. For further information contact AARP, Membership Department, 215 Long Beach Boulevard, Long Beach, California 90801.

HOUSING

Now that you are your own person, you may want to consider where and how you are living. Does the house or apartment you live in fit your needs and budget? If you and your husband put a lot of love and care into your home, you may choose to remain in it. But let that be a choice based on your present needs and situation, not on leftover loyalty. Some women find a large house difficult to maintain or feel isolated in the suburbs.

Women who live in apartments have other things to consider. Is the apartment in a safe neighborhood? Are you fearful about going out? If you are to become a person, you want to be an unafraid person.

Another possibility is to live with relatives in a duplex. When grown children do not want you living alone but you don't want to be underfoot, this may be a solution. In this way, you have your own apartment with a separate entrance but are close to a member of your family if need arises. As one woman said, "I can stay up as late as I wish, get up when I want to, and don't have to answer to anyone. But if I want company, I can call my daughter and see if she wants to talk. She feels free to do the same. It's a really good way of living."

Sharing your house or apartment with another person also offers an opportunity for companionship and for help with expenses, if you can find a person with whom you are compatible. But sharing can sometimes be disastrous. If your new housemate drinks too much or is a slob and you are very neat, the arrangement will probably not work. Consider your own needs and how they can be met most effectively when you think about sharing.

A condominium or cooperative apartment is another housing alternative. Many women find that these apartments offer them the opportunity to own property while retaining some of the advantages of apartment living, such as a security system. Besides the mortgage payment, however, there is a monthly condominium fee to cover operating and maintenance expenses. The U.S. Department of Housing and Urban Development (HUD) has a free booklet entitled *Questions About Condominiums* that can be obtained by writing to the Publications Division, HUD, 451 Seventh Street SW, Washington, D.C. 20410.

The opportunities for expanding your life are endless. They are overwhelming and frightening at first. Yet once you recognize that it is okay—to feel good again, to stop grieving constantly, to laugh and love, and to look at alternatives and choose those that fit you, you may be able to say, as one woman widowed about four years did, "I am more than a widow now. I have an identity of my own."

SUGGESTED READINGS

Abarbanel, Karin, and Siegel, Gonnie M. *Woman's Work Book.* New York: Warner Books, Inc., 1977.

Bolles, Richard N. *What Color Is Your Parachute? A Practical Guide for Job Hunters and Career Changers.* 5th rev. ed. Berkeley, Calif.: Ten Speed Press, 1978.

Komar, John J. *The Interview Game.* Chicago: Follett Publishing Company, 1979.

Lenz, Marjorie, and Shaevitz, M. J. *So You Want to Go Back to School.* New York: McGraw-Hill Book Company, 1977.

NRTA–AARP. *Your Retirement Activities Guide.* Long Beach, Calif.: NRTA–AARP, 1978. (215 Long Beach Blvd., Long Beach, Calif. 70801)

Chapter 13

Some Special Problems

This book has been written to offer some answers to questions most often asked by widows. Obviously, not every question that each widow asks has been answered. In this chapter, I'd like to touch on some that I was unable to deal with in the rest of the book. These are some of the out-of-the-ordinary questions that you may have thought about. The answers will not be extensive, but they will give you some feeling of the infinite variety of human experience.

THE UNHAPPY MARRIAGE

In previous chapters, I talked mostly about marriages that were satisfying. The husbands and wives may have had differences, may have had quarrels, but were basically able to resolve their difficulties and viewed their marriages as happy and normal.

What about the unhappy marriage? Consider the marriage between a man who drinks to excess and a woman who goes along trying to change or help him, unable to detach herself even though she is unfulfilled in many ways. When the drinker dies, does the widow mourn? Or is she, perhaps, relieved because an untenable situation has been resolved without her having had to do anything?

What about society's expectations of the widow that the widow cannot meet? What about the marriage that was a mistake—maybe not one that either spouse realized at the beginning because they were both young and society said to get married. So the young man of thirty marries. He wonders, at the altar, what he's doing there, but there is no one to tell him. Whom do you talk to when you are young and you are attracted to someone and she wants to get married—and it's the thing to do?

As the marriage continues, they both realize it may not have been the best thing for them. They grow apart, but they have children, do all the things that young married couples do, and are unhappy. Then he sickens and dies. It may be a lingering death or a quick one. She's left with what—grief? Or relief that the marriage is over and there was no messy divorce?

There is still loss. There is still grief. No one can have an intimate relationship and not feel loss at the other's death. The loneliness is there, but there is also relief. For now you can live your life as you wish—no more destructiveness from the drinker, no more silences from the husband with whom every communication meant anger turned inward.

Since almost half of all marriages now end in divorce, there are surely many unhappy marriages that do not end, for whatever reason, until one of the spouses dies. The problem for these survivors is that their feelings, which are valid, are even less accepted by society than those of the grieving widows. So these persons experience intense guilt for having feelings that are very often realistic.

DEATH OF A DIVORCÉ

What about the marriage that ended in divorce, and then the former spouse dies?

I recently counseled a woman who did not understand why she was grieving for her ex-husband. She had been divorced fifteen years earlier, and she was remarried. When her first husband died, she felt intense grief at the loss. Her feelings frightened her.

My counseling consisted of allowing her to experience the grief as a valid feeling. The divorce had not been one characterized by hatred. Her husband had visited their children often. Her relationship with him had been comfortable. Although she had let go of him as a spouse, her emotional attachment was still there, at least partially, and her reaction was one that I found normal. However, she received no reinforcement from society, which was embarrassed by her show of emotion for a dissolved relationship.

By accepting her emotional pain, she was able, after a couple of months, to come out of her grief.

SUICIDES

What about the widow whose husband has died by his own hand?

For the woman whose spouse takes his own life, the feelings described in this book are intensified by the guilt she may feel. The fear that she was somehow responsible plagues the survivor of a suicide. I have listed some selections in Suggested Readings at the end of this chapter for this widow.

THE INSTITUTIONALIZED SPOUSE

What about the woman whose husband is in an institution? She has none of the privileges of a widow, though she lives like one. Wouldn't she find his death a blessing?

I recently talked to a woman whose husband has been in a mental institution for three years. There is no hope for his ever attaining normality because he has brain damage and is virtually a vegetable. This woman considers herself a widow, but society views her as married. She is under pressure to conform to society's expectations while her husband vegetates and she marks time. I am sure she will be relieved when her husband dies. She has mourned for the last three years. Other women whose husbands vegetate in nursing homes with no possibility of recovery go through a similar experience.

IN-LAWS

How about your husband's family? How should you relate to them?

In our society, there are no formal ties with in-laws. When your husband died, your relationship with your in-laws became ambiguous. Some women have maintained good relations with in-laws and have told me that their mothers-in-law, sisters-in-law, or brothers-in-law were very helpful and supportive. On the other hand, if there were conflicts with in-laws during the marriage that were kept in check for the sake of the marriage, these may surface after the death. Often, the expectations of in-laws are excessive. You may be asked to enshrine your husband when you are trying to let go of him emotionally. It may be a while before a balance can be reached between your needs and those of your in-laws.

On the other hand, in-laws may badger you to remarry if you have young children because they feel the children should have a father. They do not place your needs first. In this kind of situation, it is important for you to firmly but gently express to your in-laws that, although you appreciate their concern about the children, *you* will decide when and if you remarry. Keeping your own balance is the most important issue.

MOTHERS

Some mothers want their widowed daughters to move back "home." A widow whose mother is living may find that her mother reassumes a maternal role that does not recognize the widow's adult status. The ultimate manifestation of this attitude is the mother's suggestion that the widow move back home, even though the daughter has lived a very separate life with her husband. Often, the widow will need to reassert her independence from her parents. She needs to break away. It may seem a hard thing to do, but it is necessay if she is to live her life as a person, not a child.

COMPLICATIONS

There are many possible complications of normal grief. These include physical and emotional illness, delayed grief, and exaggerated emotional reactions. A person often overreacts to a loss because of previous losses. The person may become stuck in grief, unable to recover even after years.

If you feel you are having problems with grief and have been unable to resolve your feelings over a period of time after seeking the help of friends and relatives, then seek professional help. If you feel your alternatives are too limited or you think about committing suicide a great deal and these feelings persist, seek professional help. Finding an appropriate person to talk to is important. Check with friends and relatives about whom they suggest. Make an appointment for an evaluation first.

In your discussions with a helping person, you need to feel trust and support. If you do not, it may be that the helping person is not the right one for you. You will need to find another professional who understands you.

One woman who sought and found excellent professional help spoke of her relief. She said, "Finally I knew I wasn't alone. Someone was going to care about me."

SUGGESTED READINGS

Cain, Albert C., ed. *Survivors of Suicide.* Springfield, Ill.: Charles C Thomas, 1972.

Faberow, Norman L., and Shneidman, Edwin S., eds. *The Cry for Help.* New York: McGraw-Hill Book Company, 1969.

Frederick, Calvin J. *Dealing with the Crisis of Suicide.* Public Affairs Pamphlet no. 406A. New York: Public Affairs Committee, Inc., 1972. (381 Park Ave. S., New York, N.Y. 10116)

A Final Note

Widowhood is one of the most profound experiences a woman will face.

Once widowed, you come to grips with your own mortality. You, too, will one day die.

By coming to terms with the finite nature of life on this earth, you begin to live your life in the present.

Enjoy it!